Conversations
With Mary

Blessings!
Barbara Harris

Conversations With Mary

Modern Miracles
In An Everyday Life

Barbara E. Harris, R.N., B.A., HNC
Illustrated by Ruth Höök Colby

Heron House Publishers

Manufactured in the United States of America

Library of Congress Catalog Card Number: 99-71659

ISBN: 0-9670406-0-4

Illustrations and cover art copyright of Ruth Höök Colby

Cover design: Pearl and Associates

Selections from *The Prophet* by Kahlil Gibran, copyright 1923
by Kahlil B. Gibran and renewed 1951 by Administrators CTA of
Kahlil Gibran Estate and Mary G. Gibran are reprinted by permission
of Alfred A. Knopf Inc.

Heron House Publishers
P.O. Box 1449
Osprey, Florida 34229

Dedication

This book is dedicated to our children, their mates, and our grandchildren. They fill my life with joy and love.

and to

"My Auntie Mame"

She was always there for one and all
A smile, a delightful laugh I do recall
Though many knew her not as well
She was my sun, my sea, my shell
Oh God, whose Spirit writes this poem
I know you've taken your loving servant home.

In Memory of the Special Love We Shared—11/21/02-1/3/99

Acknowledgments

I wish to thank my husband for his constant love and devotion and his patience while helping me with the computer. Without his assistance this book would not be.

I also give special thanks to my many friends and professional colleagues who encouraged me to write this book about the Blessed Mother Mary, and to Doctor Richard who assured me that these communications, though extraordinary, were within normal limits.

A special note of thanks to Ruth Höök Colby for her artistic visions and for her unfailing belief in this book, and to her husband, Bob, who so willingly shared his time with this creative endeavor.

And last, but most importantly, my appreciation to Chip Harris and Laurie Rosin for their hours spent editing this manuscript. It is because Laurie, a professional book editor, thought my writing to have merit that I continued with what began as a short story.

Contents

Foreword

"When I find myself in times of trouble, Mother Mary comes to me." Although these words were written by John Lennon in 1970, they could have been written by my wife, Barbara Harris. *Conversations with Mary* is a book that contains compelling stories of mystical, spiritual events.

I worked many years in the left-brain world for a large corporation. My marriage to "Bobbi" twenty-three years ago started me on a path that led to the magic of unexplainable synchronous events in my own life. This journey accelerated following a successful bout with cancer and ultimately led to a position as an interfaith hospital chaplain. It was while serving the dying and their families that my own spiritual experiences reached a pinnacle. I am now able to understand and appreciate the events related in this book to which I was a witness and participant.

It has taken much courage for "Bobbi" to write this book. I watched as she struggled *not to write* some of the words that seemed to be "sent" to her. Yet in the end she achieved the telling of a miraculous and unusual life story. The theme of Mary as the Universal Mother and a call for a return to caring and compassion are more than evident. I recommend this book to people of all religions and faiths as a book about unconditional love.

LINTON (CHIP) I. HARRIS JR. MBA, BEE

Madonna of the Window

Looking at the window this Christmas Day,
You have come to me now in another way.
Oh, Lady of Fatima, why pick me?
Though known to me since I was three,
Mary, why do you speak to me today?
I wonder aloud as I start to pray,
Am I worthy to tell this wondrous tale?
What will the outcome be… and I pale.
Mary, how did this ever happen to me?
You know they rarely mentioned thee.
When I was taught about Jesus and God,
Why did they leave you lain beneath the sod?
"I'm not Catholic," protesting, I said.
"I'm Jewish," she replied. "Get that in your head.
Go on, brave heart, bare your soul today,
And on their knees, many more will pray.
For God is in you, is everywhere seen—
In the villages and cities, in the children's dream."
"O, Mary, Mary, afraid am I!"
"Hush now, my child, don't you cry,
For I will protect you. I'll pave the way.
All that's required is a prayer each day.
"Oh, Mary, Mary, what if they give me drugs?"
"They won't, my child. You'll receive many hugs."
"The last time your crucifixion, your Gethsemane.
"This time your heaven. . .for you are free."
Your guardian angels are standing true,
And an archangel is sent just for you.
Michael will lead you. Do not fret
As throughout the world this message is let.
Put it forth once again as before. This time you're rocked
in my arms evermore."

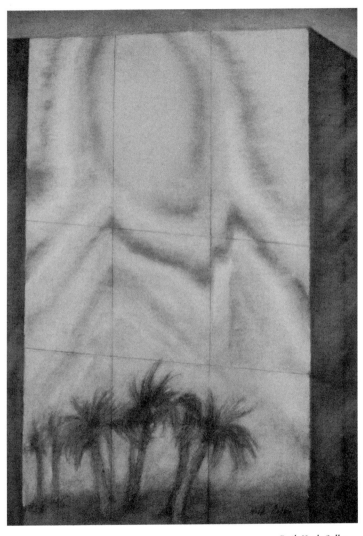

Ruth Hook Colby

Madonna of the Window

.

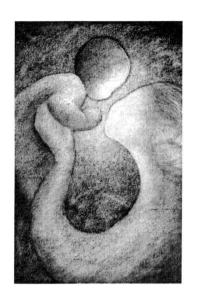

Chapter
One

Our Lady of Clearwater 1996

*D*ear *Mother Mary*, I prayed fervently, *will you pro-tect me if I publish my stories?*

And her reassuring reply: *Don't be afraid, my child. Tell your stories.*

Please send me a sign, I pleaded. *It has been more than thirteen years since you appeared to me. Won't you please come again?*

Just a few days later I was astonished to hear the words of the announcer on the evening news.

"Scientists are still searching for an earthly explanation for the forty-foot-tall image resembling the Madonna that has appeared on nine sections of a smoked glass window in the Seminole Finance Building on December 17th," the television newscaster reported, with amazement clear in his tone.

I stood in the family room and watched, stunned, as television cameras swept over the thousands of visitors gathered that evening. I remembered that it had been just a few days earlier that I had asked Mother Mary for a sign. *Steady,* I thought. *Don't let your imagination run away with you.* I stood, motionless as if glued to the spot.

"The infirm, the faithful, and the hopeful have all come to Clearwater, Florida, this week before Christmas," the reporter continued. "The Associated Press has reported that almost half a million people have flocked to see an image on a financial building said to resemble the Madonna. The building's owner has no explanation for the Virgin Vision, but he acknowledges that an incredible artist and divine intervention must have played a part in creating this glorious image of the Virgin Mary."

Hearing this broadcast took my breath away. My hands began to tremble and my heartbeat quickened. My husband and I were planning to have our annual Christmas Day dinner with my son, Erick, and his family in Palm Harbor, just a few short miles from the Clearwater building. The fact that a visit to the site of the image would be a convenient side trip did not escape my notice. Was this a divine coincidence?

I believe what Carl Jung, the noted psychologist, taught: There are no accidents. He described a phenomenon called synchronicity. It occurs when two simultaneous events that we call coincidences are related in a profound way that is not casual. These events command our attention or may even change our life. For me, the image in Clearwater was a synchronous event.

Could this image of the Mother Mary be a demonstration for me? I wondered. *Can my stories be so important to mankind that the Blessed Mother has made this appearance?* I mused.

"I don't think so!" I said out loud with certainty, and yet my excitement and curiosity increased as I thought about asking my husband to go to Clearwater.

I tried to trace the genesis of my special, comforting relationship with the Blessed Mother Mary. Neither the Baptist church I attended for the first twelve years of my life, nor the small neighborhood Methodist church I belonged to thereafter, emphasized Mary's role. I certainly was aware that Mary was the mother of Jesus and I do remember saying "born of the Virgin Mary" during the Apostles' Creed spoken on Sunday morning. However, her role was minor compared to the revered status she holds in the Roman Catholic Church.

Suddenly a clear, sweet memory came to mind. I was a little girl of about three years old. I picked up a statuette of Mary from my aunt's beautiful manger scene at Christmas time and kissed it. I did not want to let it go and they had to pry it out of my hands. Odd that I remembered that incident these many years later! I wondered if my soul had been hinting at the depth of the relationship I would have with Mary decades later.

The evening I heard the broadcast, I tentatively broached the subject of going to Clearwater with my husband, Chip. I told him about people claiming the appearance to be a vision of Mary and learned that he had already heard about it on the car radio. I asked him if he knew where the image was located. I was amazed when he readily produced a map and showed me the spot. In fact, he had already considered the possibility of a visit. I was very surprised that he had an interest in seeing the image.

I did not say anything to him about my prayer and its possible connection to Mary as I thought he would think it ludicrous. Our youngest daughter, Amy, visiting for the holidays, would be accompanying us on the journey. I did not confide in her either.

On Christmas Day we drove along U.S. 19 toward the finance building. At first, the city streets seemed normal. Then, suddenly the traffic slowed to a crawl as we approached the building. As we inched forward, I lowered the car window to see if I could see the building or the window. I saw nothing. Then the pace quickened.

Adrenaline surged through me as a traffic cop stopped our car to allow streams of people to cross the highway. He grinned at us through the windshield, and my husband rolled down his window.

"Merry Christmas!" Chip called. "Quite a crowd, hey?"

"It's unbelievable, " the young officer said, laughing. "We're expecting twenty-five thousand people here today."

We parked the car in a large lot across the street, then joined the throng at the side of the building where thousands of people could gather at one time. Awestruck crowds were staring up at the immense darkened window brought alive with the rainbow image of the Blessed Mother Mary. I was unprepared for the rush of emotions I experienced. For me, this image required neither faith nor imagination to look like the Madonna. It was not a shapeless form. Brilliant sunlight, streaming across the nine, large-paned windows, clearly outlined the motherly figure in luminous color. I was astonished, and the sanctity of the moment took my breath away.

For days the newscasters had been treating the vision lightly, but not one scientist had yet been able to explain the formation of this heavenly shape. It was thought that minerals in the water had created the distinct silhouette, but how? *Had the mineral, water, and glass experts come forward?* I wondered.

All around me, reverently silent children and adults knelt on the asphalt. Some made the sign of the cross over their tattered T-shirts or exquisite holiday finery. Most people clasped rosary beads in hopeful hands. I became extremely aware that I was not a Roman Catholic and also acutely aware of the importance of Mary in the lives of others. Then the thought came to me that *I did not have to be Roman Catholic to honor Mary as the Universal Mother.*

The melodious sounds of Spanish, French, and Italian blended beautifully with the crisp New England and soft Southern accents. Metal wheelchairs and wooden crutches intermingled with exquisite emeralds and dazzling diamonds. No one seemed conscious of status or apparel. We were the people of faith and hope, all coming together this Christmas Day in this spiritual moment—all believing in the unseen side of life. *We are all one!*

I peered ahead to a makeshift altar where candles of all colors and shapes flickered dimly in the bright sunlight. Nearby, on a drab, gray concrete wall in front of the windows, an ordinary, small cardboard box held donations for All Children's Hospital in St. Petersburg, Florida. Single roses, pink and red, and small bouquets of brightly colored flowers—some plastic—were scattered on the wall. A red poinsettia or two were casually placed on the ground.

The holiness and reverence of the moment were palpable in the air. Continuing to look up at the image and expecting to be unimpressed, I was stunned by my reaction. My breath was momentarily taken away, my heart began to beat rapidly, and the hair on my arms stood up straight. A large chill ran up my spine as I stood transfixed. I consciously centered myself and took some deep breaths. *Now don't get carried away,* my objective self said. *Look at this rationally.*

Suddenly, I heard Mother Mary's nurturing voice reverberating in my heart. It was as if a tape recorder had been turned on. The clarity and sweetness of the sound took me by surprise.

It has been said that I would come and give messages to the planet, she said. *I have come to Clearwater, Florida, because the name of the city is significant.*

21

This is an important part of my message. **You must have clear water.** *The pollution of the water must stop. This is not an option. This is necessary for the survival of the planet. The seas and the oceans are your lifeline.*

It is no coincidence that you are here this day, the blessed voice continued. *I have chosen you as a vehicle through whom my message will be spread. For many months you have been debating whether to accept this assignment. This is my last call to you. You must tell of this day and of our previous meetings in a book.*

In that sacred moment, my heart overflowed with love. My eyes, brimmed full with tears, now spilled over onto my winter-tanned cheeks. Unashamed, I let them fall freely. Deeply moved, I suddenly did not care what other people might think of me. I looked up at the Blessed Mother and silently said, *Oh, Mary, I don't know whether I have the courage to tell of our hallowed meetings. I am so afraid of ridicule.*

Yes, tell your stories, she lovingly urged. *Let it be known unto all the people, for they are stories about the sacredness of all life. This is not a question of religion. Those are man-made—it is a question of faith and souls being denied access to the body. All individuals must be responsible for their actions. To do otherwise is to wreak havoc on the earth. You must tell of the miracles of birth and the choice of adoption. This is my message to you: Put forth your book for all whose eyes are open to see,* she said with finality.

The voice fell silent. I was overwhelmed and left speechless by her message. Me? Write a book! I did not know how to write a book. Who would publish it if I wrote it? But deep in my soul I knew I would obey her mandate. I would write the stories of my most closely held family secrets.

Following this message on Christmas Day, I tried to behave as if nothing unusual had happened. Though uneasy, I decided not to tell my family members for fear that the sacredness of the moment and Mary's message might be lost to me. However, I was bursting inside to tell someone. Later in the evening, when we returned home, I recorded her message and shared my experience with my husband. Although he was an engineer and computer scientist by education, he had been led into a hospital chaplain's training program following a bout with cancer. After almost a quarter of a century of marriage, he was now accustomed to my frequent intuitive experiences and was encountering synchronicity in his own life.

"I had something extraordinary happen today in Clearwater," I hesitantly told him. "I received a strong directive from Mary while standing in front of the window. I have recorded the mandate she gave me. She told me to write a book about her visits to me through the years," I continued.

His response was nonchalant but supportive. "That sounds interesting. It would be quite an undertaking. I accept the stories because I was there, but are you sure you want to publicly go out on a limb like that?"

"If I don't crawl out on a limb, how can I taste the fruit?" I replied, rather annoyed. "I don't know what to do," I continued, the anguish now evident in my voice. "Mary told me to write the book, so I have to trust that I will be shown the way!" I said with bravado. I was not sure that I knew how to write the stories nor whether I wished to share them with the world.

For years I had suppressed the extraordinary events surrounding my two hospitalizations and the adoptions of one daughter and then my firstborn grandson. My rational mind warned me to keep my secrets, and the prospect of going public upset me because privacy—my own and my daughters'—was of the utmost importance to me. Because of Mary's mandate, I obtained permission from my daughters to tell their adoption stories. Nothing stood in my way now but my fear of disclosure.

I realized that I had no choice. Because Mary had played a major part in guiding both these adoptions, and my hospitalizations, I knew that I must follow her directive. I could no longer deny the role that the Blessed Mother played in my life.

In the next few months, my life slowly changed. I saw fewer friends and spent more time in prayer and contemplation. Our social life dwindled to almost nothing. I began to sit at the computer to write about my experiences with Mary. The computer was a challenge because my husband had installed a new software program and I did not know how to use it. I was often very frustrated and unable to work when he was not home to answer my questions. Soon, I began to dread the time spent at the computer; I intensely disliked mechanical things. The stories would languish idly in the computer, unread and unedited for weeks at a time.

I was now completely overcome by the formidable task of writing a book. The fear of going public was increasing and I began to have bad dreams about it. What would people think if I said that Mother Mary was appearing to me? Would they think I was delusional?

I continued with my busy private holistic nursing practice, but even that brought reminders of my book. The first client I agreed to see for a home visit had an exquisite oil painting of the Virgin Mary over her bed. Two paintings of ethereal angels flanked the central painting. My client, a talented musical director, had

brought these paintings from Italy where she had conducted a choir for the pope. My client asked me to visit
her friend who was also very ill. Her friend had three
adopted children. *More synchronicity.* I could not escape
the message. The burning desire, the nagging voice, the
constant knowing that I must write would not go away.
Still the stories remained untouched.

A full year passed before any news of the Madonna of the Window, as I now called her, would be
sent my way. A friend called me about an article she
had seen in the *Venice Gondolier*, a small Florida newspaper. She had an idea I was going to write a story about
my Clearwater visit.

"Say, didn't you tell me that you and Chip went to
see the image of Mary in Clearwater?" she asked.

"Yes, we did," I answered.

"Well, I'm going to send you an article I just read
about that," she continued.

"Oh, that will be great! I'm interested in reading it," I
replied, trying not to sound *too* interested.

In truth, I *could not wait* to see what the story said.

When I read the article I was upset. According to the
newspaper, the building had been leased to the Ugly Duckling Car Sales for company offices. I sure didn't like the
name. Perhaps there was some significance in the children's
story that would turn this miracle into a beautiful swan.
Perhaps, like the ugly duckling, this vision of Mary was in
its infancy and would mature into an international shrine
for her. I prayed this would happen.

The article further stated that scientific experts
now say the discoloration in the glass panes was caused
by a chemical reaction from the watering of shrubbery.
I was not satisfied with the explanation of the appearance. Why did this chemical reaction not occur in a

pattern on the matching windows on the other sides of the building? How was it possible for the distinct pattern to continue between the large panes that reached up more than forty feet? How did the water reach a height of forty feet? Why is the form forever embedded in the window panes that rise up three stories high? These are the questions the scientists could not explain.

The most fascinating piece of information in the article was about a Fort Lauderdale stockbroker interviewed on site who thought the image to be an *abortion* statement. Reading that, I got a chill and the hair on my arms stood up. He pointed out that the Virgin image appears on nine panes of glass, each representing the nine months of pregnancy. He further stated that the image faced the abortion clinic that was just a mile down the street. I sure did not want to get embroiled in that controversy!

After reading the updated article, I felt that my message received from Mother Mary a full year earlier to be even more valid and important. It now seemed imperative that I complete my book. My determination intensified and I made plans to close my private nursing practice to free up the time I needed.

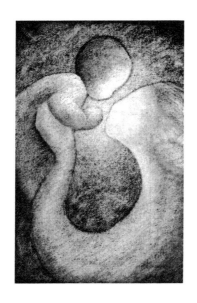

Chapter
Two

Mary's First Miracle
1968

In 1963, my first husband, John, and I miraculously survived a serious automobile accident. Following our recovery, John suggested we have another child. I was surprised but quickly consented, with one stipulation—that we have at least *two* more children. Our first three children, ages five, six, and seven, enjoyed a wonderful camaraderie, and I did not want to raise a lonely "only" child, separated from older siblings by a significant age difference.

The timing was excellent. John's medical practice was thriving and Erick, Andy, and Allison were in school full time. In 1964 we had a darling baby whom we named Michael. When he was approaching his first birthday, I was looking forward to having another baby. It was not to be, however, for a routine pap test revealed that I was in the early stages of cancer. The gynecologist recommended a hysterectomy. Devastated, I scheduled the surgery. So my hopes for a sister or brother for Michael were dashed.

Once my recovery was complete, my husband and I discussed adopting a baby girl. I called agencies across the United States. Some told me to forget it because we already had four children. Some people laughed. Others suggested we seek a child from a foreign country.

A strong, intuitive "knowingness" that my little girl was somewhere out there, waiting just for me, kept my resolve strong. I was especially sure of my quest when I prayed. Each evening before going to sleep I said the same prayer: *Thank you, God. I know my little girl is coming soon. Keep her safe.*

Always the same message returned from that small voice inside, *Have faith, she will come!*

After two years, I lazily said this prayer about once a week. One evening, I distinctly heard a woman's voice reply. *I hear you!* she said in exasperation. *It is done!*

The voice startled me. When frightened, I often use humor to deflect the anxiety. *Is God a woman?* I asked myself . . . and laughed.

Suddenly a clearly defined vision of Mary, the mother of Jesus, appeared before my eyes. She wore the familiar blue garb: the colors were vivid, her countenance was lovely. She radiated love and looked just like the paintings I had studied in college in my art-appreciation course. In the vision, Mary carried a baby wrapped in a pink blanket. As I watched in amazement, she reached out as if to hand the infant to me. Frightened, I sat upright in bed. The vision did not disappear.

Mary, I asked timidly, *is it really you?*

Yes, it is I, she responded. *Have patience.*

At once the picture faded. I was astounded but felt very indignant. *Mary, you don't know what patience is!* I thought angrily. Then I felt ashamed of my preposterous and arrogant response. My momentary shame turned to elation. A bit frightened, but very excited, I woke up my husband to tell him of this extraordinary event. He was very upset and cautioned me not to tell anyone. He insisted that it was just a dream. But I knew it was *not* a dream. I *knew* that adoption was just around the corner. I *knew* a divine plan had been set into motion. I believed it with all my mind, heart, and soul. My second daughter was coming!

But nothing happened. I called back the many agencies and all my networking contacts. They offered no hope. Weeks grew into months, and my thoughts of adoption faded. Occasionally my eight-year-old daughter, Allison, would prompt pangs of longing when she asked, "Where is my little sister? I thought you said she was going to be born soon."

"Someday, darling," I replied. "When God wants us to have her, she will come." I truly believed that.

Raising four active youngsters kept me very busy. I did not have much time to think about adoption. Yet, many nights I fell asleep thinking about the picture of Mother Mary handing me a baby. Some nights I would lie awake, after all was peaceful, and think about the sudden appearance. *Why would Mother Mary come to me?* I wondered, then decided that Mary was the universal symbol of motherhood and passed it off as an association that my mind had made.

During this time I was attending a small Methodist church. I briefly thought about talking to my minister about Mary's visits, then quickly abandoned that idea. These were definitely not ecumenical times. Mary was barely mentioned in our church liturgy, and more than one Protestant church organist had been reprimanded for playing *Ave Maria.*

In fact, I had wanted *Ave Maria* sung at my wedding, but my mother told me that it could not be because it was a "Catholic hymn." Now I wondered what prompted my request. I was then twenty-one years old and had never been taught to revere Mary. Perhaps my love of that aria also foretold of my future association with Mary.

The months turned into years. My days were busy caring for my children and studying at a nearby university. My plans were to combine my nursing education with a law degree. God had other plans.

One night my youngest sister, Carly, and her husband, Vince, came over for dinner and, on short notice, brought along two new friends. Carly and Vince were very special to me—I had introduced them on a blind date. Their friend, Kate, was lovely—tall, impeccably groomed and fashionable, with laughing green eyes and radiant auburn hair. Joe was handsome—tall, dark, with warm, dark-brown eyes. They were obviously in love.

Conversation quickly disclosed that Kate had served as a nun for more than twenty-five years, and Joe had been a parish priest. They had fallen in love and left their religious orders. They were now waiting for permission from Rome to be married. As the evening progressed, our dinner conversation came around to my adoption search.

"Oh, Barbara," Kate said excitedly, "I know a wonderful attorney who handles private adoptions." She removed a small red address book from her smart, black leather purse and gave me his name and phone number. I took the card and casually put it in my pocket.

"I'll call him tomorrow. Thank you, Kate."

After retiring that night, John and I didn't even discuss the information received from Kate. We were both tired from the long week and fell soundly asleep. I was awakened abruptly at about 3:00 A.M. by a tugging at the sheet and the nightgown covering my arm. I turned on the light and looked around but saw nothing. I turned out the light. Then I noticed a very bright light dancing over the paper bearing the attorney's name and address, on my bedside table. It was not behaving like a normal light. It was a brilliant, incandescent gold color.

I watched, fascinated, but for some reason, felt very scared. *Stay logical*, I told myself. *Look around for reflections. Was the light coming from the street light outside? No, it was not.* The light continued to dance as if having a life all its own. I lay still, not daring to breathe. Suddenly, the words of a little hymn I had learned as a child in Sunday school came to me, and I began to sing them very, very, softly:

> Brighten the corner where you are.
> Brighten the corner where you are.
> Someone far from harbor
> You may guide across the bar.
> Brighten the corner where you are.

The bright dancing light promptly disappeared. I took this as some sort of indication or divine sign that I should call the attorney. With that thought, a chill ran up my spine.

The next morning I decided not to tell my husband about this incident. Any mention of Mary's name upset him. Schooled in medicine, he was very uncomfortable with my metaphysical experiences to say the least! After I informed him of Mary's first appearance, his harsh words, "Just forget it! It must have been a dream!" still resounded in my head. But I could not forget it. *I knew it was not a dream.*

This morning as he ate his breakfast, he suddenly started singing "Brighten the corner where you are." I audibly gasped and dropped a spoon in the sink where I was standing. My husband seldom sang and certainly not while reading the newspaper and having his first morning cup of coffee. I knew from my psychology studies that because I had sung out loud, however softly, that it increased his chances of doing this. But he was definitely not the singing type. And what an obscure song to sing. I took this as strong confirmation that I should follow up on the attorney lead given to me by Kate.

I could hardly wait for John to leave for the hospital. I called the attorney as soon as I was alone. I was not into "magical" thinking so I steeled myself against the disappointment that might follow. The attorney was not in but his secretary agreed to mail us an adoption application. I completed it quickly and said this small prayer as I mailed it.

God, please find my little girl.

Once again I was hopeful, but the attorney never called. *Another false lead*, I thought, and finally surrendered. For more than *three years* my efforts had been in vain. **This is it, God! I give up! I will not try to adopt a child ever again,** my thoughts screamed.

My children were all in school now. Michael, four years old, would attend morning preschool in the fall, and I would pursue my law degree full time. The lovely vision of the Madonna handing me a child now seemed like a far away dream.

It was 1968. These were turbulent times. It was the summer following the assassinations of Senator Robert Kennedy and Dr. Martin Luther King. More than half a million American soldiers were fighting in Vietnam. Antiwar sentiments were running high. These events tore at my heart and soul. How does a young mother explain the shooting of our leaders to her children? My older children expressed confusion and fear and asked if we would be shot, too. Nothing I seemed to say could offer my children solace; nothing but my faith in God could prevail during these dark days.

One day Allison asked, "Do you think they shot our baby sister?"

I felt as if an arrow had entered my heart.

"No," I replied calmly, "I know she is safe, wherever she is."

My disappointment, the assassinations, the war, the killings, caused me to question whether I believed in God and even whether God existed. I began to doubt everything I had been taught in church. Once, while taking my nightly walk, I cried openly for being a fool and letting my imagination run away with me.

Where is my little girl, Mary? I trusted you to bring me my baby.

Soon it was summer vacation. The children and I began our annual, magical few weeks on the New England coast, where we owned a small cottage. We all loved the beach. Often I would go for solitary walks in the evening. The sounds of the water and the sight of the far flung stars made me feel at one with God. It felt so good to be tranquil.

On our vacations, I brought along the children's favorite baby-sitter, Crissi, a mature, sunny sixteen-year-old who had been my helper for four years. Her assistance gave me time to rest, to read, and to take long strolls on the beach and forget the pain of world events. I hoped that during the quiet times I would find peace with the little girl I would never know. The seed that Mary had planted still resided deep within my soul. Still, I tried to ignore the hurt and release the hope that I would find my little daughter.

The very first evening of vacation I sat alone at the water's edge, hugging my knees and rocking. Under the stars, watching the light dance over the dark ocean waters, I felt very close to God. Thoughts of the little baby girl crept into my mind once again. Why couldn't I just forget her? Suddenly I felt angry at my innocence in having believed that Mary appeared to me or that she was the divine contact between my baby girl and me. Hadn't she sent an ex-nun to give me the person's name who would find me the child?

"Oh," I moaned, "what a *stupid* little fool I have been!"

God, why don't you leave me alone? I asked, anguished. *Why won't these thoughts go away?*

The answer came from the still, small voice within. *Have patience. We are testing your resolve.*

"I don't want my resolve tested, okay?" I shouted. "Forget it! I'm done! I don't believe in anything anymore. I need to be shown!"

Looking out over the horizon, I was astonished to once again see the outline of a motherly figure, holding a babe in her arms.

"Oh, no!" I began to cry in frustration.

Shaking my head in disbelief, I looked again. The vision came into sharp focus. It was the Madonna. She was dressed in her traditional blue robe. In her arms she cradled a baby.

"Are you real?" I asked.

She did not answer.

Her serious countenance changed now to a sweet smile. Gazing down at the baby, she kissed it on the forehead, then reached out as if offering the babe to me. The image disappeared, and I was tearful. I felt deeply disturbed and frightened that something must be wrong with my mind. I could not tell my husband as he often joked derisively about "my vision."

Please God, I beseeched through tears, *help me!*

I quickly left the beach and went back into the house and climbed into bed, under a fuzzy summer blanket. I could tell no one about the episode.

Have faith. That was the thought passing unbidden through my mind. "Be quiet. Please leave me alone," I moaned and eventually cried myself to sleep.

In the morning I awakened refreshed, as if the tears had cleansed my memories. I took my older youngsters, now eight, nine and ten, to the beach. Crissi stayed behind with four-year-old Michael, who was more interested in playing with his toys than in flying kites at the beach on this cool, windy August day.

I sat watching the children launch and fly their colorful box kites. I felt so thankful as I looked at their strong, tanned bodies.

Thank you, God, for my children, I prayed quickly. *How selfish of me to want another child.* When I said those words I experienced a tug in my chest that felt as if a butterfly were flying out of my heart. I still cannot explain this distinct feeling.

At that precise moment I heard Crissi calling me. I turned and saw her running toward me, half dragging Michael.

"Phone! Phone! Mrs. B., come quick!" She was screaming and laughing in excitement. "Someone's on the phone who says your baby daughter has been born!"

"What?" I screamed. My heart was beating fast.

"A baby! A baby!" Crissi kept yelling, and Michael was jumping up and down in excitement.

My thoughts were racing. What? Who? How?

I ran to the house. By the time I answered the phone, I was breathless, and my voice and hands were shaking.

"Hello, Barbara! This is Tom McKenna, the attorney from Florida. Your daughter was born just about two hours ago. I know it's been some time since you heard from me, but we've had a run of boys born."

"Some time!" I said loudly. "Some time!" I repeated incredulously. "It's been *two years!*"

"Do you still want to adopt a baby?" he asked calmly.

My emotions were on a roller coaster. The tears were flowing, and the sobs sought to escape. I composed myself and answered evenly,

"Well, I'm going to have to talk with my husband. He won't be here until the weekend."

"Oh no, you better call me back by tomorrow morning at nine," he warned. "I've a long waiting list."

"All right," I said.

I probably can call you back in ten minutes if I can connect with John, I thought.

I immediately called his office. "Sorry, he's not here. He's delivering a baby," his nurse said efficiently.

"Have him call me as soon as possible."

"Is something wrong?"

"Oh, no, just some family stuff."

Within thirty minutes the phone rang. Quickly I informed my husband of the news. I carefully did not mention Mary.

Knowing this was my fondest wish, he acquiesced readily. "I'll fly to Florida to pick her up this weekend, if that's okay with them. Find out if you need to be there."

"Oh, but I want to go!" I responded.

My husband prevailed and devised a very practical plan so as not to disturb the children's vacation. He convinced me that they would resent their new baby sister if she interrupted their summer fun. I could hardly wait to call the attorney, but a small intuitive voice advised, *Stop, wait!*

Contrary to my impulsive nature, I decided to sleep on it and call the attorney in the morning.

Crissi and I could barely contain our excitement. Our broad smiles and giggles that evening were picked up by my oldest son, Erick. "What are you and Crissi laughing about, Mom?" he asked.

"Oh, girl stuff," I replied casually.

"I think you have a secret," he persisted.

"We do," I admitted, "and I will tell you about it in a few days."

Erick agreed not to say anything to the others about the secret, but shortly thereafter, Allison and Andy came bounding into the living room.

"Mommy, Mommy, tell us the secret," Andy, my number two son cried out.

"In a few days," I answered. "Why don't you and Crissi go out for ice cream?"

"Yea! Yea!" they shouted in response, and moments later they were racing out the door.

I was alone at last and had time to gather my thoughts. I was still reeling from the news. A baby! Another daughter! Already born.

"Oh, Mary! How could I have doubted you? I am so grateful." My thoughts raced as I thought of a newborn's needs. But something was wrong. My intuitive nature was sending me a very unsettled feeling. In fact, I was uneasy at my core. I decided to go for a walk on the beach and pray about it. I walked for a mile or so before finally returning to the house. The uneasiness persisted.

At eleven o'clock, the household was silent, and I called my husband.

"Something isn't right," I told him. "I'm not feeling good about this baby. In fact the thought of adopting her is nauseating me."

"What?" he shouted, his frustration clearly coming through now. "You've waited years for this day!"

"I know, but something's wrong," I added lamely. "I don't know how to explain it."

We quickly said our good-byes.

"I'll call you tomorrow," I said sadly and replaced the phone on the cradle.

What is the matter? I asked myself. Then the answer came. I just did not feel that this child was my daughter. *You're a fool,* my rational side told me.

Near midnight, I went out in the moonlit night to the water's edge and placed my feet in the cool salt water. All the beachfront homes were darkened. The sky was a deep midnight blue and the stars sparkled brighter than I had ever remembered. The only sound was the surf lapping on the shore. I was alone with my thoughts.

I sat down on the cool, hard sand and hugged my legs as the emotions of the day caught up with me. Placing my head down on my knees I gently cried. "What is the matter?" I asked myself. I knew my discomfort had nothing to do with having to give up my plans to attend law school. I believed I would give up a law degree in a heartbeat to adopt my baby girl, but every time I thought about doing so, I felt sick.

Please, God, I prayed. *Please tell me what to do.*

As I gazed out at the horizon a clear vision of the head of the Blessed Mother Mary appeared clearly before me once again. She was draped in a dazzling white headpiece, and the stars seemed to dance around her head in a circle.

Your daughter is yet to be born, she said firmly and distinctly.

What? I cried out to her in pure frustration. But she had already faded from view.

I do not pretend to understand how or why these appearances of Mary occurred, but my heart told me immediately that the message was correct. A peace passed over me as if an angel had caressed every cell in my body.

This was the "peace that passeth understanding," I decided. This was divine intervention, and I was *not* going to adopt this child. As soon as I reached that resolution a sense of harmony pervaded my soul.

I left the beach for the house, still weeping silently for the child who would not be known to me . . . yet mindful of another mother's joy at receiving the unknown baby. I also then became aware that there was another mother, the biological one, undergoing severe pain at the loss of her child. I prayed for her also.

"Okay," John said, resigned and rather fed up, when I called him with my decision. "You have to raise her." At that time, I did not know how prophetic that statement would be.

A profound sense of relief, followed by intense sadness, occurred as I placed the call to the attorney.

"Congratulations, Mommy," McKenna's secretary said sweetly when I identified myself.

My heart plummeted. I did not respond. The attorney was exasperated with my explanation that I sensed something wrong with adopting that particular baby.

"Nothing's wrong," he said rather annoyed. "A pediatrician and a neurologist have examined the baby. She is perfect!"

My heart leaped, but I remained steadfast. I would definitely follow Mother Mary's directive.

"We have another woman in labor," he added as an afterthought. "If she has a little girl, do you want us to call you?"

At that moment an electrical shock ran through my body. It was so strong that I was physically knocked about a foot from the spot where I was standing. My heart beat wildly. Suddenly a vision of Mother Mary appeared in the kitchen!

This is your daughter! she said, and instantly faded away.

By now her appearances did not frighten me and I was taking for granted Mary's directive again. I dared tell no one but every cell in my body knew. This was my rightful baby.

This was the soul who had chosen our family to support her during her lessons here on earth.

"Yes," I said to McKenna, "yes, yes, that is my baby. *I know it!*"

"Don't get your hopes up. A lot of baby boys have been born here lately," he said grimly.

I *knew* this was a little baby girl, just as I had known the gender of my other children and had picked out their names before they were born.

I could hardly endure the wait. Time was dragging. I made the beds, did the dishes, dusted, vacuumed the house, did laundry. I did anything to stay busy. My mounting excitement did not allow me to read, so I tried to work a jigsaw puzzle then a crossword puzzle, to no avail. I could not leave the telephone, so I paced back and forth from the living room to the family room. In those days I smoked, and I began to chain smoke cigarettes. My abdomen and lower back were hurting. I felt as if I was in labor. I suddenly realized that in all the excitement I hadn't told John what was going on. I placed the call.

"Whatever you say," he said. He was rather disgusted with my change of mind and quickly hung up the phone.

Finally, the phone rang. My heart raced.

"Barbara, you have a beautiful healthy baby girl." McKenna's enthusiasm was clear as he added, "She is just perfect, a gorgeous child."

"This is wonderful! Oh, so wonderful," I repeated, crying. "Oh, thank you, dear Mary, thank you. Please have her examined by a pediatrician."

"Of course," he said. "If we find any problems, I'll call you back right away."

"Okay, but no matter what, she is my daughter," I said vehemently. Even if something was physically or mentally wrong, it didn't matter. I was certain that I would adopt this child.

John made the flight arrangements. Because he was a physician, he was allowed to fly south to bring her home without my accompanying him. I was thrilled. I still ached to go and hold my daughter in my arms but John's pragmatism prevailed. The children were told that "our secret" was that they were going to have a little sister, Amy. They were all very excited and ran out to tell their friends.

I called my sister, Carly. She and Vince were expecting their third child. I thanked her for bringing Kate and Joe to dinner and told her the news. She was astounded and happy for me. I have seen neither Kate nor Joe since that dinner party, but I believe that Kate was the messenger and Carly and Vince were the catalysts sent from Mother Mary.

Soon my phone rang incessantly as news of the impending adoption spread over the beach. The next afternoon when I arrived at the beach front, the neighbors yelled, "Surprise!"

Pink crepe-paper streamers hung from brightly colored beach chairs and umbrellas along the waterfront. Gift boxes wrapped in shiny pink paper were piled high on a beach blanket, awaiting my arrival. This child seemed to be everyone's baby, and the women of the beachfront community spent the next four days until Amy's arrival chattering and laughing in anticipation. I could hardly contain my excitement, and sleep was nearly impossible.

I spent my next few nights by the water, communing with the stars and hoping for a glimpse of the vision of Mary. I so desperately wanted to thank her. I prayed for her to make an appearance to no avail. I was disappointed. Where was Mother Mary? Why would she not appear? I did not know.

My heart overflowed with joy, but I was also acutely aware that my joy was another woman's sorrow. I prayed for this mother many, many times, even though I did not know her circumstances.

John called from the Boston airport. "She's a little doll and a good little girl," he said hurriedly. "She took one bottle on the plane and is still sleeping."

"Oh, I can't wait to hold her," I said joyfully.

"I'll be there soon."

* * *

"She's here!" Andy called out, running to find me.

The broad grin showed his enthusiasm. He was a fairly quiet child, so his shout startled me. We all ran outside and spotted John's dark green car coming up the road. My excitement mounted, and I started to weep for joy as my husband climbed out of the car and reached back into a white wicker bassinet. I came forward, and he placed a beautiful baby girl in my arms. She was all wrapped up in a new pink summer blanket.

"Hello, little Amy," I said, cuddling her to my breast.

"Welcome to the world!"

"We have waited a long, long time for you."

"I love you!"

Her perfectly shaped round head was framed by silky dark hair forming ringlets around her face. Her cheeks were incredible! They were high, prominent and perfectly formed. She was a most beautiful baby. The exquisite turquoise eyes that she still has today opened wide and met mine in an even gaze.

It was then that a chill traveled down my spine, and the hair on my arms stood up. This was a connection felt deeply at the soul level. *I've known her before. Perhaps in another lifetime.* I had never had that kind of thought before that moment.

Suddenly a lightbulb went on in my head. Today is the fourteenth of the month! That means that Amy was born on the ninth of August! Erick was born on the ninth, as was Allison. Andy and Michael's birthdays, the fourth and fifth, added up to nine.

Was this significant? I wondered. What made me think of that then? I had never noticed numbers before, never heard of the science of numerology. But I knew now that this was more than just a coincidence—this was synchronicity.

"Let me hold her! She's my baby," said eight-year-old Allison, who stood impatiently by my side in her yellow-and-orange flowered bikini.

Placing her in Allison's arms for the first time, I thought, *my little girls are reunited at last.* That evening I rocked our little Amy and sang the same lullaby I had sung to all my children:

> Mommy's little baby,
> Mommy's little girl.
> I love Mommy's baby,
> Mommy loves her girl.

After placing Amy in her bassinet and retiring for the night, I instantly fell sound asleep, only to be suddenly awakened with a shake. There was the vision of Mother Mary once again. This time she appeared dressed in a brilliant white robe. She held forth empty outstretched arms, as if in a blessing. She was smiling sweetly, and as she faded from sight I thought I heard a baby crying.

I shook myself awake. This was no dream. It was time to get up for a three o'clock feeding. The circle was complete.

* * *

Ever since I held Amy in my arms for the first time I wondered about the strong connection between our souls. What was that momentary nanosecond of awareness and recognition that I felt when I first looked into her incredible eyes?

More than two decades later I got a glimpse of that connection. I had read *Many Lives, Many Masters,* a book by Brian Weiss, M.D., about past-life regression. The book was fascinating and as a psychiatric nurse, certified in hypnosis, I was particularly interested in his research.

I had an opportunity to meet Dr. Weiss when he was scheduled to give a seminar at a local church. After listening to his story and his research on the subject of past-life regression I wanted to experience a regression session firsthand.

Soon after, I heard about a professional in a nearby city who was assisting clients with regressive hypnosis. I had no preconceived notions about what might happen during this work; I was simply curious.

It took just one visit for me to get a glimpse of the depth of the connection between Amy and me. The therapist induced me into a deep hypnotic state; I was a willing and able subject. He then asked me to go back to the first time I met Amy. Suddenly, I was standing on a rocky shore in Alsace-Lorraine, a region in Northeast France. (It is interesting to note that I have never been to

Europe.) A large group of people encircled me. I told the therapist that I thought the time period to be the seventeenth century. A mockery of a trial conducted by a tribunal of men was about to begin.

"Who speaketh on behalf of this woman?" asked the first man.

The crowd fell silent.

Suddenly a small voice called out sweetly, but firmly, "I do."

A very little girl with long, wavy dark hair hobbled forward on crudely crafted crutches. I had healed her from a paralysis and then fashioned her crutches from tree limbs.

"Does anyone else speak for this woman?" the second man asked. There was silence.

"If no one else speaks for this woman I sentence her to be burned at the stake as a sorcerer," proclaimed a man, seemingly the judge.

It was then the little girl raised her exquisite turquoise eyes, now filled with tears, and said, "I don't want you to die."

"Don't worry, little one," I said. "I'll be with the angels."

"But I want you to be my mommy," she said. And she wept.

"I *will* be someday. Someday soon. Don't you cry," I answered emphatically.

"Who are you in this lifetime?" I asked her.

"I am your daughter, Amy," she replied.

I took my place at the stake and felt my wrists and feet being lashed to the wood with crude hemp. Then I felt the flames licking at my feet. I cried out in anguish to God.

As I began to lose consciousness a vision of the Madonna, holding a baby wrapped in a pink blanket, slowly appeared above. It was the same vision I had seen centuries later. The baby's eyes met mine in an even gaze. They were the same eyes that looked into mine when five-day-old Amy peered over her pink blanket. At last I understood that a divine imperative had brought our souls together.

I still marvel at this session. I don't pretend to understand it. I have read much research, pro and con, on this subject and it appears to have more and more validity. I only report to you my experience so you may consider it as a possibility.

* * *

Amy was born in Dade County, Florida. She is now thirty years old and living in the Northeast near her sister, Allison. She married at age twenty one. Tragically, her beloved husband was killed in an industrial explosion just weeks after their wedding. Amy, a beautiful young woman, has not remarried.

It would be two years before
Mary would visit me again....

The Littlest Angel

Sitting by the sea one day,
She visits me now in another way.
I see the vision, I hear the voice,
This time there is a different choice.
A babe held in your arms so strong
Is this the child for whom I long?
"Will she come to me yet another day?"
I lovingly ask as I continue to pray.
And then my faith brought you home,
A seed that God had surely sown.
"Where did you come from, baby dear?"
"Out of the nowhere, into the here."
Spirit has surely sent you this day!
Holding her close, I continue to pray.
Bright blue eyes gazing at me
Looking more and more like Thee.
"I came to join my family,
I bring you love through divinity.
Sent to you from the highest source,
From Infinite Mind, the strongest force.
"You thought me into reality."
My heart cries out, "Can this be?"
And clutching you to my breast as before.
My daughter you'll be forever more.

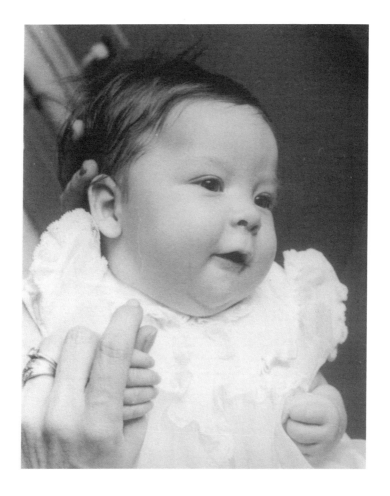

"The Chosen Baby"
Baptism, 1968

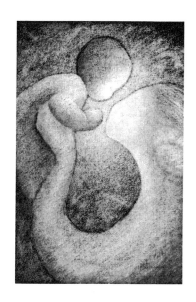

Chapter
Three

Embraced by Mary 1970

Life seemed perfect. The joy Amy brought to our family was immeasurable. Amy was now well over a year old—a darling, happy, well adjusted child. Then, it seemed that all hell broke loose. We received a phone call from the state that informed us Amy's adoption might be used as a "test case" for interstate private adoptions. We may have to return Amy to Florida where she would be placed in a foster home until the case was heard.

I began to think about clandestine plans to escape with her. I would *not* have my daughter placed in a foster home. I would risk imprisonment before that would happen. I began to have nightmares of women stealing Amy from her crib as she lay sleeping. I started to sit up in a chair guarding her crib throughout the night. I was exhausted.

John assured me he would contact the state agency and find out the circumstances surrounding the request. To this day, I still don't know the details but my husband informed me that it was "taken care of." We soon received a letter that a new judge would be hearing the adoption. I suspected someone influential had intervened on our behalf, but I would never know. Though I was delighted with the final results, the incident had taken its toll on me physically and emotionally.

The next two events occurred soon after this issue was settled. They both completely blindsided me. My young father was diagnosed with inoperable lung cancer and my husband informed me that he wanted a divorce. John cited my increasing interest in metaphysical and spiritual matters as the main reason for our irreconcilable differences. He said my encounters with Mary had "spooked" him and he asked me to never speak of them again.

At this time, I was an active member of the Edgar Cayce Society and a group called Spiritual Frontiers Fellowship, based in Illinois. Spiritual Frontiers was a lending library. About a half dozen well-worn books would arrive at a time in the mail. They made for wonderful reading during the many hours I was alone, but our marriage was disintegrating.

Extrasensory perception and precognition were now routine occurrences. I would often have knowledge of the diagnosis in emergency medical situations before the phone rang. That was a bit scary to me but the books I had read validated my gifts. John believed more and more that I was a bit "kookie," but I felt my gifts were from God. He didn't see it that way. I now realize how deeply this was ingrained in my soul and how much I feared writing of my sacred meetings with Mother Mary even to the present moment.

It was then my long, dark night of the soul began. I agreed to seek professional counseling to save my marriage but my husband was not interested in joining this effort. Only my father's illness prevented us from divorcing at this time. We hid all discussions from the family. How could I tell my parents their son-in-law and favorite doctor wanted a divorce? I could not.

These two events caused me to collapse into an undiagnosed depression. I also had excruciating chest pain. I was literally heartbroken. To me, I was losing everything—my husband and my father. I wished I had been assassinated with President Kennedy and Dr. Martin Luther King. I sought help from a new therapist, but John, as before, refused to see him.

I consulted a physician for the chest pain and was ordered a new drug called ACTH. It was cortisone—a steroid. It was ordered to quiet the exquisite tenderness and inflammation of my rib cage and sternum. I also was given Demerol, which nauseated me, for the pain, and the drug Thorazine was ordered for that symptom.

These medications were administered to me intravenously by my husband for months. They were a lethal combination and enough to incapacitate me. I literally could not stand up. I could not think. I lost thirty pounds and slipped into a profound clinical depression. I also believe I was unintentionally addicted to Demerol. Many years later the medical community would validate my theory that steroids could induce depression, manic episodes, psychosis and even suicide. That information was not common knowledge at the time. It was thus that I spent many months incapacitated in bed. My family and a nanny cared for my children.

Finally, my younger sister, Leah, came to my rescue. She worked for my husband as one of his medical assistants. One night I cried out to her in anguish and she strongly informed me that I needed to see an esteemed psychiatrist who was on the same hospital staff with my husband. However, John did not want me to see anyone from his hospital. I think he did not wish his professional colleagues to know about my illness. Nevertheless, I made an appointment to see Dr. Toltz without John's knowledge.

My visit to Dr. Toltz would turn out to be both a blessing and a curse. He struck up a conversation about a nurse, Kathy, who was under his care because she thought my husband was going to marry her. He proceeded to caution me about her. I was stunned! The wife is the last to know. And suddenly everything fell into place—that was the reason John wanted a divorce.

My expressed shock at this news alarmed the doctor. He had assumed that I knew about Kathy and he was releasing confidential information about a patient! But I felt safe with Dr. T. as I had known him professionally and socially for years. And so I bared my soul to him, sobbing about my father's impending death and my husband's wish for a divorce. And I told him the drugs were killing me.

Dr. T. asked me if I would go to a very expensive, private hospital for three weeks of treatment. I eagerly agreed as I wanted to get better. I asked my cousin, a registered nurse, to accompany me, as I trusted her. I did not want to be alone with John. I was now confused and afraid.

Just two days later I sat facing an admitting officer in one of the northeast's posh mental health facilities. The grandeur of the lawns, the glistening green waters of the palatial pools and the exquisite gardens belied what was to happen to me.

I followed the nurse down the hall as directed. What I had not anticipated was the locked door closing behind me. I was trapped and could not leave. I had naively thought that I was going to a very upscale rest home to recover and receive therapy.

I was terrified and burst into tears. This surely was the darkest moment of my soul. Though I saw the exquisite silk draperies and luxuriously thick mauve carpeting, I knew I was a prisoner. I could not leave.

People were quietly sitting in the elegant living room and talking in low voices. No one seemed to notice me as I was led by the nurse to my semiprivate room. In the other bed was a beautiful young woman curled up in fetal position. She was also in a clinical depression and lay motionless, not eating, for days. Later she would tell me her husband had only six months to live and she could not cope with this knowledge. Lying on my bed I began to pray.

Where are you now Mother Mary? I pleaded. *Please come to me now,* I begged.

But she did not appear. And I wept throughout that day and night.

I was not prepared for what was to come. The medication I was given initially caused me to pace up and down. I could not sit still nor stop talking. It induced an agonizing manic-like state. I felt as if bugs were crawling and biting me under my skin. I thought that death would be a welcome guest. That medication was soon discontinued.

The next day, as I sat in the living room during visiting hours, I heard a buzz at the locked door. A nurse in a crisp white uniform took out a large ring of keys and opened the door. A tall, beautiful young female visitor entered the room. Her long brunette hair cascaded over her slight shoulders. She wore a long natural-colored gauze dress and brown thong sandals. In her arms she carried a dark-haired baby wrapped in a pink summer blanket. The blanket was identical to the one we wrapped Amy in to come home from the hospital. Seeing the baby brought tears to my eyes.

Crossing the room she approached a handsome, young, bearded, male patient sitting nearby. He gave her a kiss and quickly began to strum a guitar and sing. I wandered closer and took a seat to listen. Looking up, he invited me to sing with him. Oh, how I loved to sing! I began to harmonize.

He suddenly looked at me with warm, shining brown eyes and said "Hi, my name is Joseph and this is my girlfriend, Mary, and our daughter, Amy!

My thoughts were jolted! *What! Joseph and Mary with a baby named Amy . . . am I really losing my mind? I don't believe this,* I thought to myself.

"Is that true, are those really your names?" I asked her.

"Yes, those are our names," she answered demurely.

The significance of the names and the pink blanket now took on a very important meaning for me. I felt this was a not-so-subtle message that somehow Mother Mary knew I was here. She was watching over me. I also realized then and now it was an unbelievable coincidence.

I listened to Joseph play a few songs. He seemed rational to me. During a pause I asked "Why are *you* here?"

"Oh, I don't want to go to Vietnam, so I'm pretending I am crazy," he said candidly. He then leaned close in a confidential manner. "I have a message for you, " he said in a whisper while looking around suspiciously. Then, leaning forward, he looked deep into my eyes and said, "The Virgin Mary said she is with you always. Shhh! Don't tell anyone," he added hurriedly.

My mind, even through the haze of the drugs, was blown! He then began to strum "Hey Jude, don't be afraid..." on his guitar and sing to his little daughter, Amy. Was I going crazy? How was it possible for this young man to give me this message? I don't know to this day.

Unfortunately, I did not heed his words. When I was interviewed by my assigned physician, he questioned me over and over about "religious delusions" intimating my husband had made reference to them. I decided to be completely truthful and tell him of my encounters with Mother Mary. I shared my story about Mother Mary's guidance during Amy's adoption. Having checked the names of Mary and Joseph with a nurse and had them validated, I also told him about the message the young man gave me. I was seeking a professional explanation. What a *mistake!*

"How do you explain that?" I asked him pointedly.

The doctor was visibly uncomfortable and agitated by my question.

"I don't explain it. You are both very mentally disturbed," he answered in a disdainful manner.

Then tenting his hands in a superior gesture, he informed me gravely:

"I am ordering nine ECT (electro-convulsive therapy) treatments to remove your delusions and depression. You will receive these on Mondays, Wednesdays and Fridays. I assume that as a nurse you know what shock treatment is."

"Do I know? Of course I know!" I answered in alarm. "It is barbaric! It should be outlawed! You are trying to destroy my memory!" I now shouted in fear.

Horrible scenes of patients convulsing during my psychiatric nursing affiliation at the state hospital flashed quickly through my mind.

"No!" I screamed, "I will not sign the consent form."

"Oh, we don't need your signature," he responded chillingly. "Your husband has signed the consent and we will commit you if we have to."

That devastated me. John had never mentioned this in his phone calls to me. To say that I was terrorized would be a gross understatement. Was this really the United States of America? I felt as if I had somehow been transported to a foreign country where an individual had no rights.

"No! No! I do not want my memory destroyed!" I screamed and screamed in terror. . . remembering patients who did not even know their names following treatment. And then I was taken away to my room by two large men and forcibly sedated.

I heard the ECT cart roll down the gray and peach marble hall. It contained the instrument that would administer thousands of volts of electricity to my brain and would cause me to convulse. I could hear it coming like a slowly moving monster. It would then stop. . . do its dastardly deed . . . and then slowly begin to roll again toward my room. The sounds of the wheels were louder and closer and I knew I would be next. I felt as if I was waiting to be electrocuted—as if I were on death row. I was curled up in a ball and whimpering in terror like a puppy. The medical team entered. My whole body was now shaking uncontrollably in fright. I tried to calm myself.

Breathe deeply . . . you are going to be all right, I told myself. And at that moment a ray of brilliant light containing the colors of the rainbow appeared through the window. For me this was God's way of saying, "I am here."

"Please, Mother Mary," I cried out, "I need you now." There was only silence. Then I remembered Mary's message to me. She had said, "I will be with you." So I began to breathe again fully trusting the words.

As the doctor leaned down with the medicated syringe that would render me unconscious, a beautiful vision of Mother Mary appeared over his head. She was dressed in a brilliant white robe and headpiece. A halo of stars seemed to twinkle above her head. I wisely kept my mouth shut. She reached down and encircled me in her

Religious card carried in Barbara's wallet in memory of Mary's embrace.

arms saying, *I am with you always.* And I was suddenly peaceful. I knew I could not be harmed and though I was given nine electroconvulsive shock treatments, Mother Mary appeared and cradled me in her arms every time. I now had inner peace and would never have a moment of confusion following this invasive, barbaric treatment.

After awakening from the convulsions, I joined the other patients who received this treatment. We were herded into a small room. Though every other patient had temporary or sometimes permanent memory loss *I had none!* People were so confused they were literally bouncing off the walls. My only complaint was intense muscle aches from the top of my head to the tip of my toes from the induced convulsions.

After three weeks and nine "treatments" I was discharged to home with prescriptions. It is noteworthy that this was exactly the length of time our insurance allowed. John took me back to this facility twice more. Once I was kept for five days and once overnight and sent home. He never gave me another intravenous medication and it is with delight that I report to you that I had a full, swift recovery and have never suffered a mood swing since. Our marriage, however, would never recover and John and I would eventually divorce.

In 1976 I married my present husband, Chip, and have been happily married since. John consented to Chip's adoption of Amy and it was finalized in 1983. John also remarried and moved out of state. He died in 1995.

I would not see Mother Mary
again for nine years.

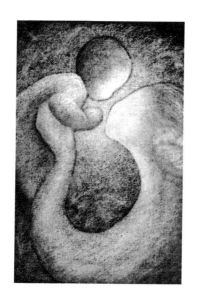

Chapter
Four

Mary's Second Miracle 1979

Mom! MOM! HURRY! Something's wrong with Allie!"

The sound of Michael's boots crashing down the stairs was the only warning I had of my daughter's crisis. I quickly left my comfortable chair and bolted up the stairs and into Allison's room.

Allison was standing, bent over, next to her bed. Her small, delicate hands were placed protectively on her melon-sized abdomen.

"Don't be upset, Mom," she said calmly, "I'm in labor. I was raped."

Her words seared my soul.

"Who?" I demanded. "When?"

"It's not important now," she said, wisely.

I had been with my nineteen-year-old daughter, Allison, almost daily for the last nine months and had no idea she was pregnant. With each question dozens of possible answers raced chaotically through my mind. Suddenly my vision blurred, my legs weakened, and my knees buckled. I was reeling, in danger of losing consciousness. *God, give me strength,* I prayed fervently.

A thought immediately entered my mind in answer. *Your strength cometh from the Lord who made heaven and earth.*

I was in awe of the immediate response. My body strengthened, and my heart and soul were filled with peace at the deepest level, enabling my training as a registered nurse to take over.

"Have you had prenatal care?"

"No."

"Okay," I said, and sorted through what needed immediate attention.

"Lie down so I can time your contractions."

The situation seemed surrealistic, as if I were split into thirds. One part of me performed professionally and unemotionally as a nurse. Another part, the first-time, excited grandmother, was also in evidence. Allison was my eldest daughter and my first biological grandchild was about to make an appearance on this earth.

Meanwhile, the third of me that was Allison's mother was in agony. My little girl, raped? She had carried this knowledge by herself for nine long months . . . going to work each day . . . listening to my admonitions because she had allowed her slim, athletic body to become plump. My heart became heavy with an exquisite ache that I believe is reserved for mothers.

Suddenly a vivid picture of Mother Mary came into my mind. I could see her face clearly as she beckoned to me. She was standing, robed in white, suspended in a gleaming golden light as she pointed to a babe cradled in her right arm. I shook my head in disbelief—she appeared to be standing right next to me.

I will be with you, her countenance seemed to say.

I was amazed and a bit shaken to see her once again! I believe the shock treatments had terrorized me into "forgetting her." These memories flooded me now and I began to weep. *Oh, Mary, thank you for coming to me again after all these years*, I cried, as I sank to my knees in reverence and grief.

I had received a beautiful gift from God with the adoption of Amy. So now did I have to give up my first grandchild to another family? Was this the law of cause and effect?

NO! NO! I screamed silently. *I cannot do that.*

Although Mary's appearance startled me at first, she was now providing comfort to me that all would go well. It was then that my pain and the sense of it became obvious. This is what Amy's mother felt like and this is what Mary must have felt as a mother—the sorrow of losing a child.

I rapidly dismissed that thought, because I knew that I was experiencing only a fraction of the pain suffered by the Virgin Mother while witnessing her son's crucifixion. I focused on Mary's greater loss and pain and used it for my own solace.

Mary, I prayed, *I am so sorry that you had to watch your son die. What agony you must have felt. How did you bear the pain? Oh, how my heart hurts for you! I know if you got through that, I can get through this. But I need your help. Please be with me now.*

As I finished my quick prayer, the glowing vision of Mary faded, but my emotional strength and courage returned.

Allison's contractions, growing stronger and lasting longer, demanded my full attention. I needed to find an obstetrician fast. I picked up her phone and called one of the nearby hospitals.

"You're lucky to get him on this weekend," the operator said, giving me the name of the obstetrician on call. "He's the best!"

My work history in hospitals had taught me that the operators knew everything about the medical staff. I

71

was bolstered by the good news, but only momentarily. As I returned the princess phone to its cradle I thought, *my little girl is not a princess anymore.* The pink phone now seemed incongruous with the unfolding events.

I called the doctor and, feeling utterly foolish, related the facts. He was very understanding and we agreed to meet in the emergency room.

I hung up the phone and walked down the stairs as if in a trance. The cozy family scene with our visiting children was incongruous with what I was about to say in front of them. "Chip, Allison is in labor and we have to go to the hospital," I said as calmly as possible.

"What?" he shouted and jumped to his feet. "It can't be—she's not pregnant," he added indignantly.

"Yes, she is and we have to go," I said firmly.

Not trusting my husband or myself to drive our precious cargo, and knowing that Allison would need professional assistance should a rapid delivery ensue, I phoned 911 for an ambulance. My thoughts were solely of Allison and how alone she must have felt while carrying her secret for nine months. I was also concerned about her labor because I had experienced a difficult first birth.

While Allison and I sat on her lovely, white, quilted bedspread and waited for the ambulance to arrive, I wrapped my arms around her and crooned the lullaby I had sung to her many years before.

> Mommy's little baby
> Mommy's little girl
> I love Mommy's baby
> Mommy loves her girl

Inane words, but the pretty tune always seemed to soothe her. "Don't be afraid, Allie," I said with false bravado. I was shaking inside.

Soon the red revolving lights of the ambulance shone through her white bedroom draperies and swept an eerie shadow across the walls and ceiling.

"I will always be here for you, honey," I said.

On the way to the hospital my husband and I discussed our adopting this grandchild. We did not have time to make the decision. As soon as we arrived at the hospital events happened quickly including a series of mystical coincidences. These coincidences would, in my opinion, convince even the most steadfast skeptic of the presence of a higher power in the universe—one I call God.

The admitting clerk was a professional young woman wearing a tailored navy blue pinstripe suit. She was very empathetic to our plight.

"Oh, how can this be? How could I not have known?" I repeated over and over as tears welled up in my eyes. I had often heard of young women carrying their babies to term without their parents knowing they were pregnant. As a nurse I never understood how that could be possible. Now I had firsthand experience. Feelings of guilt and failure swept over me as we answered the questions on the admissions form.

Having finished her interview, the young admission officer leaned across her desk and took my hand. "Everything will be fine," she said with confidence. "You and God are a majority. This is my first night on duty as a hospital-administration intern, I will personally watch over Allison and pray for perfect adoptive parents for the baby."

"Thank you . . . ," I floundered for her name.

"My name is Sister Miriam."

My eyes widened. This was the seventies, but where I came from, nuns didn't wear crisp white blouses with business suits, leather pumps, and sheer nylons. And so the magic of synchronicity began to be revealed. My prayer to Mary had already been answered by Sister Miriam's presence. Just as with Amy's adoption, a nun was to play a primary role in the adoption of my grandchild. I almost told her about Amy's adoption and Mother Mary's appearances, but decided this was not the time.

In my heart I knew that, from the many choices, Mary had directed me to this particular hospital. Convinced that my prayer was answered my demeanor became calm and sure. I accepted that I was entering a painful period of growth for my soul.

Allison was in labor all night. I stayed with her while my husband dozed fitfully in the waiting room. She and I talked softly. Her long, straight, wheat-colored hair was now very wet from the exertion of labor. As I lovingly stroked her brow and rubbed her back she, at last, confided in me as to what had happened to her.

While Allison was at a neighborhood party, one of the young men she knew had asked her to come into a bedroom to talk with him. She went, feeling perfectly safe. The idea of being raped in this upper-class neighborhood was so preposterous that it never entered her mind to be wary. These parties were held in very large homes and the average attendance was nearly one hundred people. With the noise of the conversation and the rock music blaring, Allison's calls for help went unnoticed.

"Why didn't you tell me, sweetheart?" I asked.

"After I discovered that I was pregnant, I decided I didn't want you to hurt for all those months, Mom," she explained, her almond eyes brimming with tears. "Besides, I made an appointment to have an abortion."

That stunned me, but before I had a chance to react she related the following story to me.

Her abortion had been scheduled for a Saturday morning on a crisp fall day. On Friday, Allison was waiting for the elevator in the building where she worked. The elevator cage zoomed up past her floor, then stopped, and came back down. When the doors parted *no one was inside*. But what looked like a MasterCard—orange, black, and white—was on the floor, leaning against the back wall.

"I thought someone had dropped a credit card so I picked it up and looked for the cardholder's name. But it was a facsimile of a MasterCard, and it read PUT CHRIST IN CHARGE OF YOUR LIFE.

"Finding this card was earthshaking to me. How had it gotten there? Why at that moment?" she added, pensively.

I understood her confusion. Allison had always been very alert, very perceptive and most of all, logical. As a child I took her to Sunday school and church every week, but as a teenager, she rebelled against church. I respected her right to explore other or even no religious beliefs and institutions. After she had sifted through the evidence of the existence of a higher power, examined the circumstances surrounding Jesus' birth, and asked questions about the millions of non-Christians in the world, Allison proclaimed herself an agnostic.

"I stuck the card in my pocket and planned to go through with the abortion scheduled for the next morning."

"But the card persuaded you otherwise?" I asked.

Now another wave of contractions gripped her, and I watched the heart-rate and blood-pressure displays on the bedside monitor. The readout showed that she and the baby were doing fine. When the contractions subsided, she continued with her story.

"Yes, the card and another incident," she answered. "Do you remember when we were having a cup of tea at the breakfast table and Amy got all upset 'cause of a nightmare?"

I nodded. How could I have forgotten? Amy had screamed, then ran downstairs and flew into my arms.

"Mommy! Mommy!" she wailed. "I had a terrible nightmare!"

"What was it about, honey?" I asked, holding her tightly on my lap and kissing the top of her head.

"I dreamed someone flushed me down the toilet!" she cried.

"Oh, it was so terrible."

As I thought back on this incident, I realized how devastating Amy's outburst would have been for Allison—considering Amy's adoption at five days of age.

"My heart nearly stopped and dropped out onto the floor," Allison admitted. "I was about to do to my baby what Amy had dreamed about. I was going to have an abortion. I was going to flush my child down the drain, down the toilet."

A shudder ran through her as she remembered how she had felt.

"I decided at that moment that I couldn't have an abortion. Someone or something—a power greater than I—was involved in the events and influencing them. I decided to cancel the abortion and trust this higher authority," she laughed nervously. "But, Mom, I was so scared!"

So months earlier, as she looked at her beloved little sister, with her long chestnut hair and bright turquoise eyes, Allison knew in the depth of her being that she was meant to give birth and give the baby up for adoption.

"I know you and Chip want to adopt this baby...."
She hesitated, always the diplomat, choosing the right
words. "But you have too many children now, and I think
my baby should go to younger parents."

She was right but my heart was breaking. I loved children. How could I ever give up this baby? This was, after
all, my first grandchild. But Allison's story and her decision resonated deeply within me, at the soul level. I became resolved to follow her wishes. I decided, then, not
to go with her into the delivery room. I realized that if I
saw her son—somehow I was certain that she was having
a boy—I could never let him go.

I stayed with Allison until about eight in the morning,
when she was moved to the delivery room. The obstetrical
nurses had promised me that they would call me when the
baby was born. As I watched her being wheeled away, my
heart was filled with anguish.

Why is this happening? I wondered. *Is this my
test—to give up my own first grandchild to strangers?*

My very essence screamed, *No!*

Exhausted, I went to join my husband in the waiting
room. I clung to him as sobs wracked my body. But then I
remembered Mother Mary and what she had endured. This
thought again gave me a sense of calmness and peace pervaded my soul and a feeling of courage returned.

The ride home, though just a half hour, seemed end-
less. The telephone rang within ten minutes of our entering
the door.

"A healthy baby boy," the nurse reported. "He's just
perfect and weighs a little over eight pounds. Allison is
doing just fine."

Deprived of sleep and in deep emotional pain, I was
infuriated by the nurse's cheerful demeanor.

"Fine? Fine?" I screamed silently. *"No, she is not fine, and neither am I."*

My inner voice sobbed, and the anger rose in my throat as I thought, *"I will never see this child, never rock him, never gaze at his face, nor see his eyes widen at the wonder of the newly fallen snow. NO! Everything is not fine!"*

I continued to sob deeply as I trudged upstairs, washed my face, and reached for my favorite light-flannel nightgown. Usually this gown had a comforting effect, but I couldn't sleep. Finally I got dressed and went to the real estate office where I worked as a relocation counselor—a position I enjoyed because it was a "caring profession." And it gave me the flexibility, which nursing did not, to allow me to attend to the demands of my home and children. The broker's wife, Sharon, had become a dear and understanding friend.

Getting out of my car in the parking lot, I slowly made my way to my office door. My legs felt like lead. I did not feel like being there that day, but did not know where else to go. I could not stay home. I could not look at Allison's bedroom.

Please, Mother Mary, stay by my side, I begged, tears filling my eyes.

Oh, how I had longed for this day when I would become a first-time grandmother, I wailed to myself.

"And now I will not even be able to hold him," I cried out loud. Shaking my fist at the stand of stately trees, now full with the blossoms of spring, I began to cry once again.

As I approached the steps to the back entrance to our office a shiny object, almost concealed in the grass, caught my eye. The early morning sunlight reflected a gleaming white light.

Photo by Chip Harris

Miraculous Medal
found by Barbara
May 1979.
The inscription reads
"O Mary Conceived Without Sin
Pray for us who Have Recourse to Thee."

GIVE
Christ charge
OF YOUR LIFE

Photo by Chip Harris

Facsimile of MasterCard charge card
found by Allison
September 1978.

"Oh," I thought in amazement. "I haven't seen that bright a light since I last saw Mother Mary at Amy's adoption."

I bent down and picked up the object. It was a sterling silver, religious medal bearing a picture of the Virgin Mary. My whole body shivered in recognition of this huge moment in my life. My legs became weak. I was now convinced that Mary was with me, guiding me. Allison must be fulfilling a divine purpose. Overcome with humility and awe, I sank to my knees there on the grass and prayed.

Oh, God, Mother Mary, I beseeched. *What is happening?* I then thought, foolishly, that I didn't know any Catholic prayers, so I said what was in my heart. *Thank you, thank you, for being with me in my hour of need,* I cried.

And now I could see Mother Mary clearly standing before me, again suspended in an incredible golden light. Her outstretched arms and her very presence comforted me. Her countenance full of love calmed me. She did not speak but her arms seemed to encircle me. My heart and soul were filled with a profound peace. I once again experienced the "peace that passeth understanding."

I sensed that I had stumbled on a great secret of universal law. Mary, Jesus, God, angels—they were all with me, always available to me to call on them. I now felt certain that everything about this miraculous birth had been planned and would turn out perfectly. I just did not know how or why. Even Allison's rape had a spiritual purpose. I just did not know what it was. At that moment I let go of the outcome.

With the medal of Mary clutched in my hand, I shakily ascended the stairs and entered the quiet, deserted office. I called the hospital to see how Allison was doing.

"I'm okay, Mom," she responded softly. "I named the baby Christopher, for Christ, because of the card I found in the elevator."

Her young voice sounded so solemn, sadness overwhelmed me once again. My heart leaped at her decision, which I knew was another part of the miracle's unfolding. I quickly reached for the medal of Mary that I now carried in my pocket, put it to my lips and kissed it for strength.

"That is a wonderful choice," I replied.

"I'll call our attorney and find out how to proceed with the adoption if that's what you want, sweetheart."

I was bravely saying all the right words, but my voice sounded far away, as if I were on automatic pilot.

"Okay, Mom," Allie replied. "Remember, God and you are a majority. Everything will be okay."

Oh, poor Christopher Robin, I thought after we hung up. I don't know what made me think of that poem at the moment. I sat looking through the office windows toward the building across the street, where our attorney rented his professional suite. *Poor Christopher Robin. Poor Christopher Robin.*

Those words replayed themselves as I lay my head on my desk. Thoroughly exhausted, physically, mentally, emotionally, and spiritually, I dropped off to sleep.

"Barbara? Barbara, are you all right?" A soft hand touched my shoulder. It was Sharon. Because of our friendship, I decided to confide in her.

"What?" she responded in disbelief. "I saw Allison two days ago. She wasn't pregnant!"

"Yes, she was."

Then, I tearfully explained Allison's decision to give baby Christopher up for adoption. I also told her that we did not wish to charge for the adoption. We would be happy if someone would just pay Allison's one-day hospital costs and the attorney's fees.

Sharon looked at me with widening eyes.

"Oh, Barbara," she said joyfully but tenderly. "I have a wonderful friend in California who wants to adopt a baby but can't because the cost is astronomical. Please let me call her."

I wanted to know everything about the couple. Sharon told me that the woman and her husband had a wonderful marriage but could not have children of their own due to her traumatic accident. She was an artist and had been valedictorian of her class. She and Sharon, both about ten years older than Allison, had been college pals.

"She and her husband are a gifted, creative couple. They would make fabulous parents," she continued excitedly. "Her husband's a great guy!"

"What does he do?" I asked.

"Carpentry, but he's going to apply to chiropractic or medical school, I think."

Oh, great! I thought. Now my imagination was really running away with me—*a carpenter, just like Jesus.*

Trusting and respecting Sharon's impeccable opinion of people, I gave her permission to contact her friend. She hurried into her office and placed the call while I put my head down on my desk and dozed again. Clutched in my hand was the religious medal of Mary. In the background, I heard faint bits of the conversation: ". . . upper middle-class family . . . very attractive. . . athletic . . . smart . . . ."

Even now it seems like a dream.

"Barbara, can you arrange for a neurologist and a pediatrician to see the baby?" Sharon was back at my desk, beaming down at me. "Laura is so excited! She and her husband wish to adopt the baby, pending the doctors' examinations."

"Laura?" I asked.

"Yes, my friend."

The woman's name is Laura? Another mystical coincidence? "Laura" was the title of the song that my now-deceased father had always asked me to play on the organ when he came to visit. Or am I going off the deep end with this synchronicity thing? I wondered. *No,* I decided. *This means that Christopher is going to his rightful new home.*

Sister Miriam had prayed with us for perfect parents. Although I knew this adoption decision was spiritually aligned with God's purpose, my tears flowed once again.

I began to think out loud. "Let me call our attorney," I said, and so the adoption of little Christopher was set into motion.

Laura and Allen flew in from California to meet with our attorney. Sharon kept me informed of the progress of the adoption.

"They're changing his name," she told me. "They're calling him Luke."

Chills and shivers traveled the length of my spine and my hair stood up on both arms because Luke had been my affectionate nickname for Allison's father.

A few long days later I was sitting in our office with a corporate client. My desk overlooked the parking lot and street. We watched as an attractive young couple got out of their car. The young woman had long, straight, strawberry-blonde hair, and the handsome young man was bearded. She carried a baby wrapped in a blanket.

"Look," my client remarked, "Don't they look like a modern-day nativity scene?"

As soon as the words left his mouth, I realized that I was watching my grandson and his new parents going to the nearby attorney's office to finalize the adoption papers.

I quickly excused myself and went into the bathroom. I clutched the sink for support as my knees began to buckle and I slowly sank to the floor. I could not stand; my grief was too much to bear. The tears now became sobs, and I heard excerpts from Handel's *Messiah* as I sat on the floor in the tiny room.

"Surely, surely He has borne our grief and carried our sorrows."

The music did not console me, and I did not even question the fact that I heard this music. I just hoped my client could not hear me sobbing. I tried to stand, but once more, collapsed in anguish, kneeling in sorrow on the small bathroom floor. Then Mother Mary again appeared to me in a golden light. This time Mary put her arms around me, pulled me to her bosom and rocked me.

It will all be fine, she promised. *Christopher is with his rightful parents now. We have been arranging this for some time. You must believe that Allison was the channel that carried the soul to his parents. All is as planned*, she continued softly and gently.

And then she was gone once again. Slowly rising from the floor I felt a sense of strength and composure. Phrases from my favorite book *The Prophet* by Kahlil Gibran, began to bounce around in my thoughts and consoled me.

"Your children are not your children."

"They belong not to you."

"They come through you but not from you. . ."

"You may house their body but not their souls. . ."

"You are the bows from which your children as living arrows are sent forth."

"They belong to the Universe."

It was then that I surrendered and accepted Christopher's adoption to be of a divine nature.

* * *

If that were the end of this story, it could be considered a wondrous tale of miracles and synchronicity. But there is more. Our lives in a small New England town provided only one-half of the equation. The other half unfolded across the continent. In California, before we even knew of them, Laura and Allen co-led a church group with another couple who were expecting a baby any moment. And Laura's sister and brother-in-law also had recently adopted a baby— a very expensive proposition. Surrounded by people who were having children, and knowing the cost of adoption, Laura and Allen were feeling hopeless about ever having a child. Then Allen had a dream. In it, a tall, bearded man in a long white robe stood holding a lamb in the crook of one arm. His other hand grasped a staff. "Allen, Allen" the man called, "you are going to have a son, and you will name him Luke."

Allen described this dream to his wife the next day. He felt deeply troubled because the dream had been so real. Although he had never had a vision, he was certain that this was indeed a materialization. Shaken, he called his minister for counseling and guidance. The men concluded that the dream had been the result of the stress Allen was feeling because his friends and relatives were having babies and because of his intense longing for a child.

Early the next morning Laura received the phone call from Sharon about Christopher's birth. In compliance with Allen's dream, they renamed their miracle baby Luke.

* * *

These two interweaving stories certainly provided all the miracles for a wonderful tale of synchronicity. But there is more. When my husband and I were married, we found a

Ruth Hook Colby

The Blessing

perfect home to accommodate our family. Unfortunately, because of its location, Allison, then seventeen, was forced to transfer to a new high school for her senior year. She accepted the situation and, making the best of it, became determined to win the position of starting right wing on the girls' hockey team. This was an ambitious goal because her new school held the state championship and had a very strong team.

On the day Allison and I went to the high school to register her, we walked past a beautifully painted athletic mural that including a young girl playing hockey. The girl held a hockey stick in her hand, and her long, straight, golden hair lifted from her shoulders as she ran toward the goal.

"Hey, Allie, here you are," I said, somewhat startled, because the resemblance to my daughter was uncanny.

She stopped and stared at the mural. "Boy, Mom, it really does look like me," she agreed, laughing lightly.

We learned later from my friend, Sharon, that the mural artist is Luke's adoptive mother, Laura, who graduated from that very same high school many years before.

Mary, I thought, *you are perfect.*

Allie went on to be the starting forward on the hockey team. Her team captured the state championship once again.

Not surprisingly, I think often of those hours and days that profoundly influenced me. The circumstances surrounding Christopher's birth and adoption gave both Allison and me a gift of unshakable faith and showed us the unseen side of life in all its splendor.

For nineteen years I have carried the MasterCard that Allison found in the elevator and the religious medal of Mary pinned inside my wallet. I hope some day to give them to Luke.

* * *

A decade later, Allison, happily married, gave birth to a son. It was then that I felt vindicated for not having realized that my daughter was pregnant ten years earlier. Allison never needed maternity clothes for her second pregnancy either. Both babies weighed more than eight pounds. Chip and I were once again with Allison for her labor and birth. This time, however, our grandson's birth was a very joyful occasion.

Allison has now been married for fifteen years to a wonderful man. She works as a corporate manager with the same Fortune 500 company where she first discovered the MasterCard. Both her son, now ten, and her husband are Roman Catholic. When my grandson made his first Holy Communion, I was unable to be there. The pictures Allison sent me of the procession just *happened* to be snapped when he was walking by the statue of the Virgin Mary that stands in front of his church.

Four years passed before Mother Mary and I would meet again...this time on her turf.

Christopher Robin

Oh, little one just newly born
Who from her womb has been torn
I will never see your baby face
Never know nor feel the grace
That God has bestowed on you.
Christopher Robin will you ever know
How much I want to hold you
Will you ever know how much I miss you
Will you ever know how much I love you
My little bird, I'll think of you each spring
Whenever I see a robin nest.
I know your mom loved you so
She gave you up to have the best.
My firstborn grandchild you will always be
So very, very special to me.
No matter what you are called
No matter where you are lain
No matter when you come,
For I will see you again.
It may not be here on this earthly plane
Nor under skies of blue
But you and I have met before
And underneath the pain I bore
I knew you were not mine
But here for someone else divine.
Baby Christopher, will you come one day
To see me when I am old and gray?
If not, we will meet again to pray
In another time, another way.
I give you up with joy and pain
You were not to be an earthly gain
But a soul that was carried by one who knew
You were neither hers nor mine to view.

Ruth Hook Colby

Letting Go

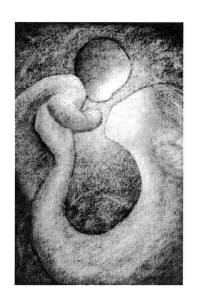

Chapter
Five

Meeting Mary
1983

$\mathcal{A}$ baby! A darling cherub smiling at me, and I reached out for him. It was Christopher. Just as I was about to hold him someone snatched him out of my arms. It was at that moment I awakened from an interrupted dream with severe chest pain. It was also then that everything went black and I reawakened in an ambulance. My husband, Chip, had called the rescue squad when he was unable to rouse me.

As I lay there in the ambulance I felt frightened and alone, out of control and powerless. A nurse for decades, I was not prepared to be a patient in a hospital. Always analytical, I tried to find reasons for the pain.

Was the severe pain from my broken heart because my first grandchild had been given up for adoption? I thought so. An early fan of Dr. Louise Hay, the noted metaphysician, I knew heartbreak could convert to physical pain, even though four years had passed since Christopher's adoptive parents took him away.

When I was wheeled into the emergency room I would tell Dr. Mason, the cardiologist on call, about my dream of Christopher. He would, I was sure, confirm my theory. Dr. Mason was a friendly young man in his late thirties. He was handsome with a Huck Finn look. I thought he would look more at home with a fishing pole than a stethoscope. I immediately liked him.

I explained my dream and chest-pain theory and the connection to the loss of my first grandchild to him. He quickly dismissed the idea. Rather than empathizing and exploring the family's loss of Christopher, he admitted me to the hospital at once for further heart testing. This was the small community hospital where Christopher was born and I had not been there since that day. My present experience was not lessening my grief.

"I had a patient just like you last month," he said repeatedly, as if trying to convince me I was wrong to connect my emotional and physical pain. "She's also a nurse, same symptoms, same age, and her arteries were completely blocked. You know, she even looks like you. We saved her life."

He was so certain of his diagnosis, he went ahead and reserved a bed in a large city hospital nearby where heart surgery was regularly performed.

"I am not that nurse!" I cried. "I am me!" My protests fell on deaf ears. I was not a happy camper. I talked once more to Dr. Mason about my theory of the etiology of my chest pain.

"You're in denial," Mason solemnly informed me. "Denial is common among nurses. You think you're invincible!" he added.

"Why won't you listen to me about Christopher?" I pleaded.

Then my rational, medically trained mind took over. I decided perhaps something *was* wrong. At my relatively young age. I knew it was rare, but I certainly *could* have blocked arteries and heart surgery *would* save my life. Though still reluctant to accept the medical possibilities, I surrendered.

I know you are in charge, God, I prayed. I *know this is for a reason. Please protect me during this procedure.* An answer came back in the small, loving inner voice I had known since childhood: *There is a higher purpose for this holiday hospitalization,* it said simply.

Trusting implicitly in the answer, I signed the legal release form. I did wonder what that higher purpose might be.

I remembered remarking to my husband a week earlier that I felt suspended, but calm, waiting for something to happen. It was a feeling I had never experienced before. Was the hospitalization what I had intuitively anticipated, even though I was enjoying excellent health?

"Anything is possible," I answered myself, and picked up a book to pass the time while I waited for the test.

But my peaceful wait was not to be. I was suddenly gripped by a wave of anticipatory anxiety. Every muscle in my body went into spasm and it felt as if I was wearing a suit of armor. In retrospect I think I was "armoring" myself for the heart catherization.

I rang for the nurse. She appeared quickly, but acted very annoyed.

"What's goin' on?" she asked, while roughly picking up my arm to check my pulse.

"I don't know. Maybe I'm having a reaction to the medication you gave me." I answered. By now my body was painfully arched backwards and my feet were reaching for the back of my head.

"I'll call the doctor right away and have him order a muscle relaxant or a mild tranquilizer," she said sharply.

"Okay, but it seems to me some drug must be irritating the central nervous system," I said.

"Could be," she answered brusquely and left my bedside.

What is the matter with her? I thought. *She is so nasty and short of patience.* When she returned with my medication I asked her if she was feeling stressed from the large number of critically ill patients in the unit. I wanted her to know I understood—I had walked in her shoes.

"No," she replied sadly, "this is my first evening back on duty in almost six weeks. My seventeen-year-old daughter went into a coma from mixing alcohol and drugs at a party."

Oh, how my heart went out to her as she sadly said, "the doctors don't think she will ever come out of it."

My concern for her took my mind off my pain and the nearing heart test as she popped in and out of my room during her shift to talk about her daughter. It was then I realized that we all have spiritual tests on the earthly plane. I was not alone in my grief. There were others with more to grieve than I. At least Christopher was alive and with a good family. I was sure God perfectly placed this nurse with me to again demonstrate that lesson.

After my restless night, a hospital aide brought me to a small room in preparation for the cardiac catherization. A friendly nurse helped me onto a black table that was cold and hard. I could hear the operating team scrubbing their hands. I was scared silly. I had not been in a hospital since I received shock therapy. As I looked around the room, I noticed that the walls were painted my favorite, peaceful sky blue. I then noticed rows of musical tape cassettes that were stored in a wooden holder against the opposite wall.

"I love music," I said to the nurse readying me for the test.

The doctor suddenly appeared next to the table and began a lively conversation.

"So you like music. Do you have the old Mario Lanza Christmas recording? It is my favorite. How 'bout Tennessee Ernie Ford and Perry Como?" he asked in rapid-fire succession.

"Yes, I have them all. I like Nat King Cole the best," I replied. We laughed, enjoying the musical memories and the camaraderie.

"Would you like some music played during your procedure?" the nurse asked.

"You bet. I would love that," I answered.

"What do you want to hear?" she asked.

"Oh, why don't you pick out a tape?" I answered sleepily. "I'll enjoy anything."

"You trust my judgment?" she asked playfully.

"I sure do," I responded in kind.

"Okay, here we go," she said, sliding the selected tape in the recorder.

The small room was soon filled with the dulcet tones of Johnny Mathis. I could not believe what I was hearing! It was "The Twelfth of Never," a song about eternal love. This was "our" song, Chip's and mine, and Johnny Mathis's rendition was our favorite. I was astounded by the synchronicity! My chin quivered uncontrollably and the sobs escaped.

"Barbara," Dr. Mason asked. "Tell me, what is the matter?"

My throat was so tight, I could barely answer. Embarrassed, I finally managed to explain.

"What are the odds of that song being picked?" I asked between my sobs. The doctor and nurses, peering at each other over their surgical masks, looked visibly shaken.

One nurse took my hand. "It's okay, it's okay," she said, but her words seemed more directed at herself than at me.

"No, it's not okay!" I screamed silently. I knew I had to get control of my emotions before they performed the cardiac procedure. I employed a favorite device I had developed over the years. I yelled, "Stop it!" while visualizing a red stop sign.

The doctor and the nurses jumped in alarm when I called out, but my method worked. As always, I calmed down immediately. I then explained what I had done. The eyes behind the masks looked puzzled—this was the early 1980s and it was obvious that no one in the room had heard about creative visualization.

"Do you want me to change the music?" Dr. Mason asked.

"Oh, no," I answered without hesitation. "I love this song. It's a good sign. My husband couldn't come into the operating room, so the music means he's here with me in spirit." That thought comforted me but seemed unsettling to the staff.

"Something wonderful is going to happen today," I added. "I know that my heart is going to be okay."

"Don't get your hopes up," the doctor responded cautiously, then added impatiently, "Let's get this show on the road."

"I'm ready to go," I replied, as it turned out, prophetically.

As the staff began the procedure, I listened to the music and focused on the words of the song: "love you till the poets run out of rhyme. . .and that's a long, long time." The marvelous melody and lilting lyrics comforted my soul.

"What's the date?" I asked, suddenly having a thought.

After a moment, a nurse replied, "The eleventh?"

"No," I said. "I think it's the twelfth, the twelfth of December, isn't it? What synchronicity!" I laughed enjoying the intrigue immensely.

"Barbara," a nurse said in her best soothe-the-patient voice, "it is the eleventh of December. Now get hold of yourself!"

The sedative relaxed me, and I could feel the catheter enter my femoral artery. Craning my neck to see the television monitor, I saw the tube inching up to my heart. It looked like a big worm crawling inside my body. Then the image of my heart appeared on the TV screen. This really was cool! What a privilege it was to see my own heart beating within my body.

"Look!" I called out. "My arteries are clear. They look just like a teenager's!"

They were just as I had imagined. I was thrilled.

The next memory I had was of a large, swirling black cloud of enormous power and energy enveloping me. I was surrounded by a roar similar to a freight train thundering down the tracks. The black energy encircled me, and the operating room slowly dimmed. I experienced no pain as I felt gently lifted from the table, like a child in the arms of her father.

Then I seemed to travel headfirst, with my hands outstretched in front of me, as if preparing for a dive off the edge of a swimming pool. *Like Wendy and Peter Pan*, I thought. Though tornado-like forces spun around me I felt peaceful, engulfed by love.

Lights blinked to my right and left. I wondered if they were other souls also traveling at breakneck speed down the long, dark tunnel of whirling energy. Some lights seemed stuck to the sides of this whirling cyclone of energy, rather than traveling forward.

Is that hell? I wondered, *being lodged in this tunnel, assaulted by a cacophony of sound while others soar past?*

I could not know. For me, this trip was warm, wonderful, and serene with neither fear nor pain. Wrapped in a warm cocoon of light, I was unconcerned about my destination. Cast out of the tunnel, I found myself suspended in a brilliant, loving light without dimension. Its every molecule spoke silently of love. Glorious, otherworldly colors were everywhere. Pinks, golds, mauves, lavenders, blues, greens, and magentas—all more luminous than anything I have ever seen on earth swirled around me. They, too, communicated love. I suddenly knew color would be used to heal on the earthly plane. It had been used before, yet this knowledge was forgotten.

Magnificent flowers of infinite varieties and indescribable colors were everywhere. Most I had never seen before. The rose seemed to occupy an exalted position among all of the flowers. Maybe that was because it was my favorite. I remembered thinking the use of flowers for healing was another forgotten body of knowledge.

Heavenly, soul inspiring, brilliant music seemed to emanate from the flowers. Was this possible? Music was everywhere! The term "music of the spheres" came to mind, and I understood what it meant.

The knowledge came to me that our thoughts initiate all creation, including disease, and that all memories are stored like genetic material in every cell and are passed down from generation to generation. I was told that loving touch given by a caring person can release these cellular memories.

I remember looking at Earth. It was but a small part of the picture. The planet was surrounded by a heavenly blue haze and guarded by very large angels. While viewing these scenes, I was simultaneously looking at my physical body lying on the operating table. Dr. Mason and the nurses, their voices raised, were administering electrical shock to my heart. I saw the large steel paddles being used and my convulsing body.

What is the message, I wondered? *First shock to my brain and now to my heart?* I still don't know. Everyone appeared frantic but I was emotionally removed from the scene. My physical body lying there lifeless meant nothing to me. Actually, I felt much lighter after discarding it. Although my physical body was not with me I was more clearly the essence of myself than ever before.

Incredibly, I had no thoughts of my beloved husband, my cherished children, or my treasured grandchildren. Nor did I miss them. Instead I felt that I had finally come back to my rightful place. I had at last reached home, and the understanding brought me profound peace.

Where are the angels? I wondered, looking around. *Where is heaven?* I asked no one in particular.

Heaven is in your heart, came the answer from a voice beyond.

Who is speaking? I asked.

It is I, Mother Mary, responded a firm, welcoming voice.

Somehow I was not surprised to hear her voice. I searched to connect the voice with an image. I could only see a firm jawline. I thought it belonged to a man.

Then I realized I was looking at a female whose nature was strong. The jaw slowly connected to a face. Most of all I remember the eyes. They were almost clear but at the same time, blue, green, and violet.

You must go back, she said, transmitting her words by thought. *Your work is not finished.*

No, I replied. *I do not want to go back.*

You must go back into nursing, she admonished. *You are a healer. You have been given a mission. Nursing is your forum for sharing what you have learned here.*

I gazed at Mother Mary in all her splendor. She stood tall and erect. Her facial expression the most compassionate and pure I had ever gazed upon. Her body radiated a brilliant white light intermingled with the most dazzling of colors. Mary's robe was a pale rose. I had always thought of her as wearing blue. *Why do you wear a rose-colored gown?* I asked.

She answered as if talking to a child. *My robe's color emanates from within, from my essence. There is no light reflection, as there is no sun here. The color rose represents a mother or father's unconditional love and it is the color of God's love for you. Remember this lesson. Love is the **only** thing that matters. You will go back and, as a healer, teach of love.*

Standing with her right arm outstretched, she both pointed the way back and blessed me. Her other arm encircled the shoulders of a beautiful little girl with long blonde hair. I recognized the child as the daughter of a dear childhood friend. Her death at four years of age had been extremely painful to me.

No, no, I do not want to go back, I insisted.

Go now, my child. Go in peace, she told me gently but with finality. *You will come back when it is your time.*

I will be waiting for you. I will also contact you as need requires I do so.

I don't want to leave, I begged in thought. *I am home.*

Bless you, my child, she answered and faded from view.

In the blink of an eye, I traveled with breakneck speed down through the tunnel and reentered my physical body. I remember being there for just a nanosecond. Then I left again. Considering how much I wanted to stay with Mary I was not surprised by my quick abandonment of the physical realm. I also was never one to accept the first no for an answer. Once again, I viewed the doctor and nurses applying electric shock to my heart and my convulsing body. *Stop! Oh no! My chest is going to be burned,* I shouted at them. They, of course, could not hear me.

The second trip was almost identical to the first. The tunnel, the incredible light, the magnificent colors, and the heavenly music were all there. But Mother Mary was no where to be found. Instead, I was met by a very large angel with a huge wingspan He identified himself to me as Michael the Archangel. His voice, just like Mary's, was transmitted by thought. There was no need to speak here. Later I was told this is called "an impress." His demeanor was kind but firm. He seemed to be guarding a door, but bade me to enter. I found myself in a large library that held no books but offered access to all knowledge.

The knowledge of the universe is available to all who seek it, he said in thought. He then gestured to the area off to my right. There was a room that was infinite. It had no walls, floor, or ceiling. I then understood that it was here that mere mortals could obtain information we had not learned or experienced on the earthly plane. I remember thinking that this is what Mozart had done; what child prodigies do.

Go back, the angel said. *You have much work to do.* He then vanished.

Once again, the Blessed Mother appeared above me: *I have visited and supported you during your grief,* she said. *I spoke to you during the birth of your first grandchild, Christopher. It is no coincidence he was divinely named for my son Jesus the Christ and renamed Luke by his adoptive parents for Luke, the great physician. This was all as preplanned. You must go back, my child, and complete your work. I know you are tired, but you must reenter nursing. You are a healer. You will teach about thought and the interconnection of all things.*

When you return to the nursing profession, she continued, *you will be part of a heavenly led movement. We have selected the nurses to lead the world into the next century because they have always been filled with love. Now they have been given much knowledge and will be writing many healing books. They will need the help of souls such as you. You will assist in the transition of nursing into the next millennium. Now go in peace.*

Though I heard the words, I did not comprehend their importance. Like a child being torn from her mother's womb, I reached out and screamed her name, *No, no, Mother Mary, please, I want to stay!*

Reaching out her right hand in a loving gesture, she blessed me and directed me back. She then faded gradually from view. I wept.

The next memory I had was reentry into my physical body. I saw a group of Nazi soldiers standing over my physical body performing what I perceived as surgery and

I awakened myself with a bloodcurdling scream. To this day I do not know the meaning of that vision.

"Mary, Mary! Are you the Virgin Mary?" I asked the figure slowly coming into my vision. She was not dressed in a rose-colored robe.

"No, I am not Mary," the nurse said cheerfully. "I'm Peggy and I'm not even a virgin." Everyone in the room laughed. It was clearly a relief.

"I'm not in heaven?" I asked.

"No, you're in the hospital," Dr. Mason replied.

Suddenly, I was oriented—back in my physical body. Something had hit me very hard in the chest. The pain was excruciating. I looked down and saw burns on my chest.

"Did you hit me with a bat?" I asked, still not fully oriented.

"No," the nurse replied. "You...."

Before Peggy finished speaking, I realized I had a near-death experience in that operating room. Having been on the nursing end of trying to save a patient's life, I knew the anguish Dr. Mason and the nurses had suffered.

"Oh, no, I'm sorry. I'm so sorry," I said over and over again.

"Are you all right?" Dr. Mason asked, bending over me and placing a solicitous hand on my shoulder.

"Yes, yes," I replied. "Oh, something fantastic happened to me," I said hurriedly and enthusiastically. "I can't wait to tell you!"

"Oh, no you don't!" he said suddenly thrusting his hand up in a "stop position" between our bodies.

"You just turned my hair gray! I don't want to hear about anything right now. I'm gonna sit down. I'm just so happy to see you talking."

"Well, okay," I said, disappointed but now fully understanding what fear he must have experienced. Turning to Peggy I said excitedly, "I went into a tunnel and saw the Blessed Virgin Mary!"

"I don't care where you went or what you saw," she responded good-naturedly. "I'm just thankful you're back here. You're suffering from shock. Those memories will fade," she answered while kindly stroking my head. At that moment, I wisely decided to record what had happened to me and not to discuss the events with anyone else but my husband.

Strolling over to the audio tapes, Peggy selected another tape. The room soon resounded with yet another song my husband and I played over and over while courting—"El Condor Pasa." I listened to the words, "I'd rather be a hammer than a nail. . . ."

I burst out laughing.

"Don't tell me that is another one of your songs," Peg said mockingly.

"Yes, and it's a long, long story," I said, chuckling.

"I'm going to take you back to your room now," she said as if she couldn't wait to get me out of the operating room. As she pushed my stretcher to the elevator, I suddenly remembered my earlier question. "Oh, by the way," I asked, "what's the date?"

"It's the twelfth of December," Peggy answered. "You were right, after all."

"Why did you lie to me?" I felt betrayed.

"Because you really 'spooked' us," she answered frankly. "If I were you, I wouldn't worry about anything you saw or experienced. Just remember this too shall pass," she added with finality.

A chill ran up and down my spine and the hair on my arms stood on end. I was silent with my memories. "This

Conversations With Mary

too shall pass" had been my mother's favorite saying. She had made her permanent trip to the "other side" on July 3, 1982. Before she died, I crawled into her hospital bed with her, held her in my arms, and rocked her.

Looking up at me with her beautiful blue eyes, faded with age, she said, "I just want to go home."

"Do you mean to heaven?" I asked.

"Yes," she answered. "When I say that to the doctors and nurses, they think I mean I want to go home to my house," my mother added in disgust.

Oh, how I wish I had been fortunate to see my mother during my trip, for it was she who taught me to understand that faith is more important than religion. I went over and over this event in my mind during the next twelve hours while I was required to lie flat on my back with a ten-pound bag of sand on my femoral artery.

I had survived what is now known as a near-death experience (NDE). Why hadn't the doctor and nurses wanted to hear about it? I guess a new thought or the possibility that there truly was an after life was frightening to them.

I was happy to see my husband when he walked into my room. "What did the doctor tell you?" I asked.

"Oh, he said you were fine. He said something about having to 'jump-start' you twice." Chip's face looked puzzled. "What was that all about? I asked Dr. Mason what he meant, and he said not to worry about it," he said with obvious relief.

He then reached for my hand and bent down and kissed me.

He had to jump-start me twice! What was I? An old Ford motor car! I was incensed about the doctor's casual explanation and proceeded to relate my wondrous tale to my husband. Three days later I would record it in pen for posterity. I never expected to tell another soul. The message I had received about my "religious delusions" were deeply ingrained in my soul.

* * *

Now I have glimpsed "home" and like my mother I long to return there someday. Even now as I write these words my eyes fill with tears. I still yearn for the peace and tranquillity I experienced. I long to be back in Mother Mary's presence. I am also astounded that I did not want to return back to my body to live what I consider to be a wonderful life.

As Mother Mary directed, I left my relocation job and reentered nursing. I would eventually become a psychiatric nurse to understand what had happened to me during my hospitalization.

* * *

In March of 1999 I learned that December 12th, the day of my NDE, is the celebrated Feast Day in the Roman Catholic Church, USA, to honor Our Lady of Guadalupe, the Patroness of the Americas. She is named for Mary's appearance to Juan Diego north of Mexico City in 1531. A permanent image of this vision mysteriously appeared on his mantle. There are scholars who have noticed and written of the resemblance of Our Lady of Guadalupe and Our Lady of Clearwater.

Fourteen years passed before Mother Mary would again honor me with her presence.

Meeting Mary

Traveling down the tunnel that day
Leaving my earthly body I pray
To see what heaven is about
To learn of God and Saints, no doubt
Instead a being of another kind
A woman so lovely she brought to mind
The times when I had seen her before.
"Are you Mary?" I asked at the door
"Yes," she replied countenance filled with love
"'Tis I who has given you a glimpse of above"
"Go back now," she silently bade
"Weep no more, be not afraid."
Blessing me with an ivory glove
Dismissed, now soaring like a dove
Returning to the earth once more
Beckoning again, turned away at the door.
There never can be a worldly gain
To match the splendor of the heavenly plain.

Ruth Hook Colby

The Reunion

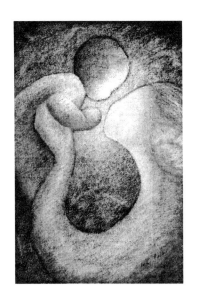

Chapter
Six

Mother Mary's Challenge 1997

It was my intention to end this small book with the story of my near death experience. But something was gnawing at me; I could not finish the manuscript as planned. I constantly thought of my Christmas conversation with Mother Mary in Clearwater and her message to me, which seemed to have two directions. She wanted her directive about cleaning up our waterways to be heard. But I was convinced —my heart told me—that the primary message she wanted me to carry forth was about the sanctity of life.

Did this mean that I would have to discuss the abortion issue? I emphatically did not want to do so. I was very comfortable, when asked about my abortion position, to answer "I am personally against abortion but I am strongly for the right of a woman to choose." It was an easy answer. It required no thought and no one challenged me. I could satisfy myself and my personal and professional friends with this statement.

But was that what I really believed? I was now uncertain.

The subject of abortion brought the completion of my manuscript to a standstill once again. I sought Mother Mary often to ask for guidance. She did not respond, so I consulted with many of my closest friends and nursing colleagues. All but one, told me *not* to take a stand on the abortion issue. Some said it would be the "kiss of death" for the book. They did not understand. For me it was necessary that I examine this issue. If I stood for nothing I would fall for everything.

One evening I prayed to the Blessed Mother Mary and there was no audible or visible answer. However, the face of Jeanne, a new acquaintance, appeared. I was confused. Jeanne is a feminist who is intellectual, well educated, well read, opinionated, spiritual and very active in a local Episcopal church. I met Jeanne socially through very dear friends, and liked her immediately.

I was perplexed. What could Jeanne possibly have to do with my book? I hadn't seen her in more than six months. It was then my inner voice told me to visit the community church that Jeanne attended. I resisted. I was wrestling with my own religious convictions. I had only sporadically attended *any* church for almost two years and I really did *not* want to do this. But experience taught me to follow my inner guidance. My husband agreed to accompany me one Sunday morning. Naturally, Jeanne was the first person Chip and I "bumped into" as we entered the church. *Okay, Mother Mary. I know you are perfect,* I thought, but I did not know the plan.

Although we did not have time to talk then, our meeting led to a social visit and a follow-up phone call. I confided to Jeanne that I was writing a book about Mary and the spiritual dilemma I was facing about the subject of abortion. Though not expressing any personal opinion, the words she said to me touched me at the soul level.

"It is no coincidence that you have called me. I have also had encounters with Mary. Bring God into your writing and you will record the words that ring true to you, " she advised. "It sounds like you have been chosen for a mission."

She had also had encounters with Mary? I was stunned! I wisely did not stray from the intent of my conversation with her.

"A mission? Me? What mission? I really do not want to write about the subject of abortion for I have to take a stand," I whined.

"It is easy to go through life not taking a stand," she said laughingly. "If you don't take a stand you don't have to think much. All the great people in the history of the world have had to take a stand. They have had to think deeply on subjects before they did this," she concluded.

"Oh!" I gulped. "I am not a great person. I am comfortable saying I am for the right to choose. I don't even know whether this is true. I have never examined the issue. I am suffering angst over this subject," I rambled on to her.

"Follow your mission," she added calmly. "Keep yourself centered in God and everything will be perfect." She spoke softly and comforting now.

That evening I went to sleep and was awakened by a vision of my mother. She came to me often. It was the anniversary of her death, a fact I was unaware of until some time later. She had two clear messages for me. One concerned my book.

Finish your book, she said simply and strongly. *Take a stand. You will be given the courage to do so,* she added. Her words reverberated in my head and soon I fell into a deep slumber.

What really is your stand on abortion? the voice asked in a challenging manner. I sat bolt upright in bed!

"Who is speaking?" I asked softly. There was no answer. I recognized the familiar voice to be that of the Blessed Mother Mary. I tried to ignore it. Maybe it would go away. Each day I heard the voice. I really was having second thoughts about Mary. I did not know she was such a "nag!" I immediately felt guilty thinking that about our wonderful universal Mother.

I could only approach my problem logically. I decided to build a personal case history of what I knew about abortion to reach a meaningful conclusion.

"When was the first time you even heard about an abortion?" I asked myself.

Case I—A Young Nurses's Choice

It was 1953. I was a nineteen-year-old student nurse experiencing my three-month rotation in the operating room. This morning I was assigned to be the first circulating nurse. That meant that I would assist the scrub nurse, who was assisting the surgeon. A registered nurse on staff was supervising me. From previous observation this would be easy for me.

I knew nothing about the patient or the case. Just enough to say hello, check for the "permission to operate" signatures and make sure that her diamond wedding ring was tied to her wrist with gauze. I thought this was to be a D&C—a dilation and curettage of the uterine wall. This procedure was done routinely for women with various gynecological problems. Although I did not know it, this morning would be different. As I stood there watching the surgeon, I saw a large piece of tissue and blood drop down into the pail. This would be mine to clean up after the procedure was over.

Everyone quickly left the room at the end of the procedure. I hurried with my tasks as another surgery was scheduled for that room. I bent down to gather the tissue for laboratory examination. When I looked in the pail the sight I saw left a scar on my soul forever. For there in the pail was a fully formed tiny baby. I could count the ten little fingers and the ten little toes. My God! I thought I would faint.

"Oh," I cried out to the air, "look at those precious little fingers and toes."

I froze in fear, nausea now overcoming me. Tears welled in my eyes and began to run down my cheeks. One of the staff nurses who was passing by saw me sitting on the surgeon's stool, crying. I was devastated.

"What's the matter?" she asked solicitously.

I could not speak but shakily pointed to the pail.

"Oh, go see the supervisor. This is a therapeutic abortion. You don't have to assist on these cases," she said casually.

"Go ahead, I'll clean it up for you," she said, giving me a little hug.

Still tearful, I sought out the operating supervisor—she was a nursing supervisor I greatly admired.

"What's the matter, kid?" she asked in her direct manner.

"I just saw a little baby in a pail and I cannot stand it," I said, chin quivering.

She beckoned me into her office.

"Are you Catholic?" she asked.

"No," I replied. "I am a Methodist."

"Then you must assist on these cases. Only Catholics are exempt."

"Then I cannot be a nurse. I will have to leave school," I said with finality.

"Oh, no, I don't want you to do that. You are going to be a great nurse. If it bothers you that much you I won't assign you in the future," she said empathetically. "I don't want any further discussion of this matter," she added emphatically while pointing her finger into my chest.

And that was that. I have never thought about this traumatic event until the writing of this book—forty-five years later.

When did you next hear anything about abortion? I asked myself again.

Case 2—A Mother's Choice

My next abortion experience happened over ten years later when I was pregnant with my fourth child, Michael. This was a much-wanted pregnancy. My husband and I had planned this baby. An early routine X-ray showed our son to be in an unusual position. His four extremities were spread out as if in a celebratory dance instead of fetal position.

My obstetrician talked with me about the possible causes. One was that his brain was open and was draining spinal fluid into my uterus. He said I had a condition called polyhydramnious; my placenta was producing too much fluid. I would have to visit the operating room periodically to be "drained" by an incision into the womb through my abdomen. This procedure was both frightening and painful because anesthesia was not administered for the sake of our child.

I talked with my husband about our options. Abortion was one. As a physician and a nurse we knew the odds of having a healthy baby.

"It's your call," my husband said.

It was then my mind flashed back to those precious little hands and feet I had seen in the pail ten years earlier. There was not even a moment's doubt for me. I would *not* have an abortion. I would have our baby. I intuitively knew Michael would be fine. It proved to be a difficult pregnancy as I could not sleep in a bed. The excess fluid made it difficult to breathe so we purchased a reclining chair. That is where I slept in an upright position for the last few months.

Michael appeared on the scene almost five weeks early on a beautiful Palm Sunday morning with an unplanned "natural" childbirth. He weighed six pounds, two ounces; a wonderful weight for an infant of this gestation period. He was a darling baby and after an initial, momentary scare he cried out proclaiming his arrival.

Were there any more cases? I mused. Yes, there was one more buried deep in my psyche. This one was obviously very painful to me and I had suppressed it.

Case 3—A Case of No Choice

It was the late 1980s. I was working as a psychiatric nurse in the dual-diagnosis adolescent unit of a famous hospital. I had chosen this specialty when Mary challenged me to go back into the nursing profession following my near-death experience. I loved the adolescents and I loved my work.

One evening I reported to the unit and the charge nurse said to me, "You don't need to listen to report tonight. I want you to special a patient in the Quiet Room, Bobbi," she added mysteriously.

"Special" meant I would sit with one patient for eight hours. I thought this unusual because the youngsters who were placed in the Quiet Room were there for disciplinary reasons. They were usually assigned to a strong, male, psychiatric technician because of the physical danger involved.

"What is the problem?" I asked suspiciously.

"Oh, it's Lorraine," she answered quietly.

"She was taken out by her parents for an 'a-b' today. She just returned and is very upset," she stated.

I was astounded! What? Fifteen-year-old Lorraine was pregnant! They did an abortion on her? My head was spinning. This was certainly no place for a postoperative patient, I thought at once. What if she hemorrhages? I quickly grabbed my stethoscope and blood-pressure cuff and ran down the hallway. Before I reached the room I could hear her screams.

Lorraine was lying on a mattress in the small, white eight by ten-foot Quiet Room. She clutched her pillow to her abdomen. Her curly blonde hair, wet with sweat, clung to her face. Periodically, she would let out an ear-piercing scream at the top of her lungs, followed by a mournful howl. "They killed my baby! They killed my baby." Then she would break into deep sobs.

I approached her gently.

"Lorraine, it's Bobbi. I'm here to take care of you," I said softly while slowly offering my hand to her.

"Don't touch me!" she screamed in fright as she crawled on her hands and knees to the corner of the room and cowered as if a frightened animal.

"Don't come near me," she shouted in fear. "I don't want you to take my baby again. Don't kill her again!" she wailed in a terrorized voice.

God, I have to do something, I thought. *But what?* I began to pray and ask for guidance.

"Lorraine, I am here to help you, " I said softly while slowly inching my way to her corner. As if in answer to my prayer, I began to sing:

> Jesus loves me, this I know,
> for the Bible tells me so.
> Little ones to him belong;
> they are weak but He is strong.
> Yes, Jesus loves me, yes, Jesus loves me.....

Where did that hymn come from? I think Lorraine is Jewish. I hope she won't mind. My thoughts were racing now. Nevertheless, I continued to sing this verse over and over very softly. Lorraine's screams gradually subsided. Meanwhile, I slowly sank down on the mattress to be closer to her.

"Why don't you come over here and let me sing to you? Come on, Lorrie, I won't hurt you, I will rock you," I said gently.

Slowly she crawled over the mattress and fell into my arms. I cradled this young child and began to sing softly. It was the same "homemade lullaby" that I had sung to my own children.

> Mommy's little baby.
> Mommy's little girl.
> I love Mommy's baby.
> Mommy loves her girl.

Soon Lorraine was quiet. Only an occasional sob escaped. "I have to check you for bleeding," I said.

"Don't hurt me," she whimpered.

"I won't," I reassured her.

I also took her blood pressure. It was very important that I have a readout on her medical condition. I was relieved that she was okay. As I finished, she crawled back into my arms and I continued to sing and rock her.

She cried and said over and over, "They killed my baby. They didn't even tell me what they were doing. I didn't even know anything until it was over," she cried weakly.

And I wept.

Her case incensed me. I sat on the floor with Lorraine for eight hours rocking her as a mother would rock a child. It was during this period that Lorraine told me she wanted to give her baby up for adoption. She had it all planned. She could bring happiness to someone else. Her life would then have meaning. This pregnancy would not be in vain. Knowing this was her wish and having been through both the receiving and giving end of adoption, I was enraged. Why did no one serve as the unborn child's advocate? Did anyone serve as Lorraine's advocate?

"No," I was informed by the social workers, "neither of them had any rights."

To me, that did not seem just. Lorraine remained under treatment in the hospital for more than a month. The night nurses reported that she would wake up screaming and crying, "They killed my baby." My heart ached for her, and for the others who would surely follow, for this was not the first nor the last teenager to have an abortion against her will. I am sure Lorraine will bear this scar for the rest of her life. Even as I write about this episode my heart is hurting. Tears sting my eyes though over a decade has passed since this event.

My soul searching was complete. In each case, *I chose life.*

I now thought my book complete, but Mother Mary had another surprise for me.

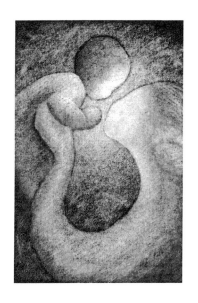

Chapter
Seven

Mary's Message
1998

One day the phone rang and I heard an unfamiliar voice on the line.

"Hi, Barbara. I'm Maya. I have received a message from the angels to call you!" she said.

I was taken aback. She then explained that she was a person who was blessed with telepathic abilities. She resided in a town close to me, but her work often took her out of state and she traveled to Boston at least once a month. She informed me that she "channeled" information from God and the angels and had been told to contact me.

"What angels? What is this about?" I asked suspiciously.

"I don't know. I'm just following orders."

"I would like you to come to see me. I won't charge you," she added.

"I have only seen a few so-called psychics in my lifetime and I really just did that for fun," I informed her skeptically.

"Oh, I just need to give you a message."

"Well, I will let you know. I'll call you back. What's your phone number?"

I really had no intention of going to see her. But I must admit her phone call caused me some consternation.

Now I had a dilemma on my hands. I was writing a book asking people to suspend their belief systems and remain open-minded. Yet, I was closing my mind to this phone call. Thoughts spun around in my head for the next few days. Why would this woman call me? Who was she? What would her message be? Would it concern my book at all? Was it possible that "angels" could give her a message to call me?

I called a knowledgeable young friend of mine to ask about this woman. My friend said that she did know of her and that she was an incredible psychic whose work took her out of state very often.

I found myself thinking about it almost every moment. After all, wasn't I open to new information? Yet I felt frightened. In the end my curiosity won out. I would go and listen. Perhaps she would have a message for me from Mother Mary. That was possible, was it not?

I called for her address and was very surprised that she lived nearby in a very upscale community. Wow! I really did have prejudices that I hadn't even explored.

It was about a week after she phoned me that I made an appointment to visit her. As I approached her door I noted her home was lovely, new and very contemporary. I rang the bell and Maya opened the door with a friendly, "Hi! Come on in!" Maya's appearance was startling. She was very tall—almost six feet—broad shouldered and stately in appearance. She was also very blonde and had a New York accent. Not at all what I expected an angel's messenger to look like.

I had a great deal of anticipatory anxiety about what was going to happen to me. She led me to a beautiful room whose glass walls gave vision to the colorful tropical flowers outside. I glanced with trepidation at the massage table that held center stage. A mauve sheet and a light blanket covered it. I felt somehow squeamish, yet safe at the same time. I offered no information.

"What are you going to do?" I asked tentatively.

"Oh, now don't worry, I am just going to tune up your chakras," she responded nonchalantly. "Come on, hop up on the table."

As a holistic nurse and teacher of energy healing, I was very familiar with the East Indian chakra system of energy. Maya closed her eyes, placed her hands about six inches above my body and began to sing in what to me sounded like an otherworldly voice. She called it "intoning." It was a magnificent sound I had never heard before, and was very unexpected and very, very powerful. As I watched her face, the muscles softened until she took on a very angelic appearance—so different from her former facial appearance, which had an I-can-take-care-of-myself look.

After about ten minutes, she began to speak. She said she was in contact with Mother Mary and her message was to finish my book. My mind was blown! Chills ran up and down my spine and I felt very cold. I reached for the blanket and clutched it for dear life.

"Have you been talking to my husband?" I said accusingly.

"No, I don't know your husband."

"Well, how do you know that I am writing a book about Mary?"

"She just told me," she answered patiently, as if talking to a small child.

I was flabbergasted, but careful to not show my emotions. I wanted to see what else she would say. I was truly astounded at this piece of information. Maya then began to pass her hands over my heart area and her whole body began to sway as if to a distant melody. Her intoning now became much louder and more melodious. My chest suddenly felt much lighter.

"You have an over abundance of 'Mary energy' in your heart," she said softly. "It is from viewing the crucifixion of Jesus."

"What!" I answered excitedly. "I think I have to leave!"

"This energy is the sweetest, purest and truest I have ever felt," she added, tears streaming down her face.

To say that I was in a state of disbelief would be an understatement. It was at this moment that I felt something warm on my right hand. I looked down to see blood dripping from the center of my right wrist. I sat straight up in the chair!

"I'm bleeding!" I shouted jumping off the table.

She smiled sweetly and replied, "That's okay. It's the release of excess empathy you exhibited from viewing Christ's death."

Now I had my clinical nursing hat on and was looking for a lesion, a mosquito bite—anything to explain the bleeding. It certainly looked like someone had punctured the center of the inside of my wrist with a small nail. Yes, I thought it was a definite small puncture wound. She covered it with a dry cloth. I held it as we sat down on the sofa.

"Why am I bleeding?" I asked again.

"Oh, that is a manifestation sent to you as you are a skeptic," she answered.

I had always prided myself on being a *very* healthy skeptic. Needless to say, I was very disturbed by the event. I quickly thanked her and left.

I wanted to rush home and show my husband my wound. It was still bleeding gently but steadily. I wanted him to see it so he could vouch that it happened. Somehow I knew I would be telling someone about it, but at the time I never thought of including this visit in my book.

Parking the car in the garage and rushing into the house I called, "Chip, Chip, look at my wrist!"

"Oh, you are bleeding! What happened? Did you scrape yourself on a nail?" he asked with concern.

"No!" I replied testily. "I went to see that psychic I was telling you about. She said Mary wants me to finish writing my book. Then I started to bleed—just like those people I have seen on TV—you know about the crucifixion," I rambled on.

"Are you sure you didn't hit it on something?" he persisted.

"NO!" I shouted loudly and began to cry. This was too much for me. I was overwhelmed.

Instead of this incident pushing me on, it slowed down my progress. It upset me and I decided to put the book on hold. Again, the insistent inner voice awakening me in the middle of the night with the same message: "Publish the book."

With my previous hospitalization more than thirty years ago, I needed reassurance that I was not "going crazy." I decided to visit a noted clinical psychologist. I would confide in him about Mary's appearances to me. Dr. Silver did not laugh at me nor think I was delusional. He validated my experiences with Mary and said that I was given a gift. I saw him about a dozen times and he worked with me to overcome my fear and accept my blessings. It is because of him I have been able to complete this book.

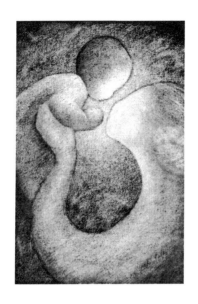

Chapter
Eight

Mary's Gift
1998

Mom, you're going to be a grandmother again!" my second son, Andy, said joyfully over the phone.

"What?" I cried in shock. The newest addition to the family would be a miracle baby. Their other sons were ten and thirteen years old. Andy's beautiful wife, Stephanie, had been near death at one point and now had a permanent colostomy. Although we did not discuss the issue, it rapidly registered with me that having an abortion because of her health problems had never entered their minds. I was delighted. It had been nine years since one of my children had a child.

"Yep, it's going to happen this spring," Andy added with pride.

We caught a jet to Arizona to be present at the birth. When I first gazed at Taylor through the nursery window his physical beauty took my breath away. Everyone at the nursery window thought he was a girl. As I stood there I suddenly realized that this was the same month and week that Christopher had been born nineteen years earlier. My eyes filled with tears.

"Thank you, dear Mary for the wonderful healing gift of this child," I prayed. I was sure she had sent me another baby in another springtime.

Taylor is a beautiful child in both countenance and disposition. When I held him in my arms just an hour after his birth he looked up at me with wise eyes in a steady even gaze that tugged at my soul. He seemed to say, "Okay, I'm here. Now get on with your book. How much *more* proof do you need?" I believe that Taylor's birth carried an imperative message.

This thought would be confirmed. Though Stephanie was aware that I was writing a book she knew little about the content. The untimely death of her mother just weeks before Taylor's birth still weighed heavily on my soul. Before we left for home Stephanie reached into a pocket and handed me a small white card.

"Here, Mom! This is for you!" she said joyfully.

As she handed the card to me I got a chill. The hair standing up on my arms told me this was a significant moment. *What is this about?* I thought to myself.

"Oh, thank you. What a cute pin!" I said. As I glanced at the card I saw a pair of tiny gold baby feet. The card said they were the *actual size of a baby at ten weeks of gestation.* My heart leaped as I gazed at the ten little toes and my thoughts wandered to the little toes I had seen in the pail in the operating room as a student nurse. Stephanie and I had never discussed that incident or shared our views on abortion. It is a subject I avoid. So, I was *sure* this pin was a message from Mary. Without further comment I hastily put it away in my purse

It was not until I was safely seated on the plane for the return trip home that I dared to look closely at the pin once again. Holding the little feet close to my heart I thanked

Andy and Stephanie for choosing to bring Taylor into this world. I closed my eyes.

Soon we had taken off and were flying at about 35,000 feet. My thoughts turned to my conversations with the Blessed Mother. I felt unsettled. Sitting up I gazed out the window at the beautiful white billowy clouds.

Mary, I communicated silently, *I feel that you want me to make a statement about abortion in my book. I don't think I can.* I waited, but there was no answer for over an hour.

Suddenly Mary spoke. *Be specific in your book,* she admonished.

What does she mean by that? I wondered.

I felt very bothered and rather irked. I did *not* want to talk about abortion in my book. I did not wish to judge what another human being did in their individual circumstance. *Judge not that ye be not judged,* came the thought.

Okay, Mary, I asked silently. *What about that phrase from the Bible?* There was no answer.

There are so many young women who have had abortions. I do not want my book to instill guilt. I want my book to provide information and be a message of hope. I mulled that thought over during the long journey home.

The next morning I had a thought as I awakened. *Wasn't it just possible that many women, like me, who consider themselves pro-choice, have no idea of what is going on in the field of abortion?* I decided to investigate the subject—something I had never done.

Okay, how do I finish this chapter, Mary? I asked, as I sat in front of the computer looking at the blank screen.

Examine the evidence, look on the Internet, she replied, clearly.

Is it possible Mary knows about technology? This seems bizarre! I thought. *But, certainly she knows everything.*

I decided to check my email before looking on the Internet. There was only one message waiting for me—from a friend in Massachusetts.

There, on the computer screen, was a story attributed to Aesop who lived about 600 B.C. I offer it now just as it appeared.

Hair We Go

A man reached middle age without ever meeting the girl of his dreams, so he never married. Then he met two women who were just perfect. One was young and had beautiful long black hair. The other, a few years older than himself, had lovely silver hair and a beautiful, peaceful manner. As this was in the days when a man could have more than one wife, he married both.

When he was with the younger lady, she wanted him to look more her age, so she would pluck out the gray hairs in his salt and pepper head of thick hair to make it darker.

However the older woman wanted him to appear more mature, so she yanked out the black hairs to create a head of silver.

After several months of marriage this man was bald.

This fable is still true today. The moral of this story is that a person who tries to embrace two opposing principles has no principles at all.

Incredibly, the words written there were: "Can someone really believe in both Free Choice and Pro-Life?

"Can someone sensibly advocate both "Concern for Children" and Partial-Birth Abortion?"

I was astounded! *Mary,* I again thought, *you are an amazing and determined woman!*

God, what should I do now? What is a partial-birth abortion? I am a nurse and I do not know as I have been in another nursing specialty. I wanted to fully understand the meaning of this term. Entering the word abortion in my computer I began to "surf the net," checking out all the related sites. What I was to find made my blood curdle. Now, Mary really had my attention! I discovered, much to my dismay, what a partial-birth abortion is.

It is important for you to know I am not referring to the removal of a child who has died a natural death in a mother's womb. That procedure is *not* an abortion. What I am talking about is the removal of a living baby, generally performed in the fifth or sixth month of pregnancy. There are also reports of this procedure being done during the seventh month and later. This is a description of the procedure:

"The baby is pulled out of the mother's womb, feet first, by steel forceps. Her torso, legs, and arms are delivered. Her little head remains inside the mother. Her heartbeat is clearly visible on the ultrasound screen. She is still moving, clasping her little hands together as if in prayer, playfully kicking her feet. She is a living baby.

"The doctor carefully leaves her little head lodged just inside the cervix which is the opening to the womb. The base of her skull is then stabbed forcefully with a long scissor or a long hollow metal tube. The doctor then inserts a catheter in the wound and removes the baby's brain with a powerful suction machine causing the skull to collapse. The now-dead baby is delivered. Physicians have said that babies at this age experience great pain and the mother's anesthesia has no effect on them.

"The difference between homicide and partial-birth abortion is a mere three inches. If the baby's head had been delivered this would be considered and recorded as a live birth!"

As a human being I was appalled and sickened by this procedure. It nauseated me. As I type the description of the procedure, I am tearful. I cannot believe this procedure is legally occurring in the United States of America and elsewhere in the world.

Mother Mary, is this why you have made your appearance to me? I asked. *No wonder. As the protector of the children of the universe I cannot imagine that you are not suffering from observing this horror. I am a nurse. All nurses and physicians have taken an oath* **to do no harm**. *I will include this in my book.*

I know that partial-birth abortion is not the most common type of abortion. Yet, I think even one partial birth abortion is one too many. If we continue to condone this procedure, we have opened the door to legal genocide of babies.

I went on to read about saline abortions performed during the first trimester when most young women have abortions. The baby is burned with the salt. Medical research has proven that the fetus is capable of feeling pain at this stage of gestation.

The purpose of this book evolved to be more than just relating my conversations with Mary during the last thirty years. My purpose is to raise your awareness of what is happening in our society today. Millions of young women are using abortion as a birth-control method. They are not fully counseled about their options, nor educated about family planning methods.

More and more teenagers, not knowing where to turn, are giving birth and abandoning their babies in public rest rooms or trash cans. Some are even killing their newborns. The teens are fearful and panic stricken. They do not know where to turn. They must feel these horrible options—abandonment or death—are more acceptable to society than giving the babies up for adoption.

The message I wish to convey is that there are more than one million couples wishing to adopt a baby today, while two and a half million abortions are performed in the USA alone.

I think we can change this situation by encouraging women of all ages, who find themselves with an unwanted pregnancy, to consider adoption as an option to abortion. We must change the perception of society so that we look upon these pregnant women as sacred vessels carrying a soul for another family. In this way, each woman who chooses to bring a child into the world can turn a "mistake" into a beautiful act of love.

I do not wish to condemn any woman who has undergone an abortion. I believe that each woman has to make her own decision based on individual circumstances. I do ask women to become informed about the pain inflicted on the unborn through abortion methods. I also ask that the present murdering of abortionists and the bombing of abortion clinics cease. These violent acts are abhorrent and are also counter to the basic principle of the sanctity of life.

There are other ways to stop abortions. We must remove the demand by responsible family planning through birth control. I offer *hope* to the next generation of young women that if an unwanted pregnancy occurs, there is an alternative to abortion and that is *adoption.*

This view of carrying a child for another family, one who has already been chosen by *God* to be the parents, is in keeping with my adoption stories of Amy and Christopher. It also matches my philosophy of nonjudgmental and unconditional love. It completes what I was told by Mother Mary in Clearwater to be my mission: *"to tell of the miracles of birth and the choice of adoption."*

And so. Mother Mary, I rest our case.

* * *

As I wrote this last line, my body was filled with a profound sense of peace and love. It was then Mother Mary appeared to me once again, descending right over my computer. Her light was brilliant, her demeanor, one of love and approval. Her right hand was raised in a blessing as she said, *At last, you've completed your book.*

With a sense of relief, I believed her challenge to me had been fulfilled and my soul's mission completed.

As if reading my thoughts, Mother Mary, standing there in all her glory, said quietly but firmly, *You have just begun your journey, my dear.*

* * *

These stories are true. Names, locations and minor details have been changed to protect identities.

Barbara E. Harris

Ruth Hook Colby

A Gift of Love

Clearwater, Florida, site as seen on March 7, 1999.

Afterword

The rainbow image of the Virgin Mary that appeared on December 17, 1996 on a financial building has not faded. The site at Drew Street and Route 19 in Clearwater, Florida, has been leased to a Catholic group from Ohio.

And so my prayer that this site would evolve into an international shrine for people of all faiths is unfolding. The blacktopped parking lot is now enclosed by a chain-link fence and chairs welcome visitors. Brightly colored flowers have been planted and a wooden kneeling bench has been provided by one of the faithful. The hundreds of notes, the rosary beads, the candles and other mementos that were left on the concrete wall have disappeared. A sign politely asks the public not to leave anything behind.

But the public *does* leave something behind that cannot be measured by science nor seen by the skeptic. The now more than one million visitors leave behind their Courage, their Love, and their Faith in the unseen side of life and they take away Hope, Peace and Strength. These are qualities not available at any price. There remains a comfort and a splendor in this scientifically unexplained vision. The important facts are these. The lovely image of the Madonna remains—it resonates with the faithful—and it is glorious!

About the Author

$\mathcal{B}$arbara Harris lives on the west coast of Florida with her husband, Chip. Together they are the parents of nine children and ten grandchildren.

"Bobbi" has been a registered nurse for more than four decades. She recently earned the coveted certification in holistic nursing. She also was awarded a bachelor of arts degree in psychology, magna cum laude in 1975, and completed holistic studies and certification as a natural health care practitioner and massage therapist in 1992. Her postgraduate studies include diverse courses in transpersonal psychology, counseling and mental health.

Bobbi has organized and served as chairperson of three national nursing conventions: "Exploring the Healing Tides," "Celebrate the Magic of Touch" and "Reclaiming Your Joy—Creating Holistic Strategies for Healing."

Guided by the Blessed Mother Mary, her personal and professional life has taken an unexpected turn in the writing of this spiritual book. Bobbi considers this book a culmination of her soul's work.

About the Artist

Award-winning artist Ruth Höök Colby uses the medium of pastel to express her vision. Her paintings have been featured throughout the United States, including "Pastels USA," at the Sacramento Fine Arts Center in Carmichael, California; the "45th Artists National" at the Coastal Center for the Arts on St. Simons Island, Georgia; and "For Pastels Only," on Cape Cod, at the Creative Arts Center in Chatham, Massachusetts. In Florida, her work has been shown at the Park Shore Gallery in Naples, the Venice Art Center in Venice, the Manatee County Cultural Alliance in Bradenton, the State Capitol Building in Tallahassee, and the Sarasota Visual Art Center, the Unity Gallery and New College in Sarasota. Ruth was born in Chicago and has lived on the west coast of Florida with her husband, Bob, for the past twenty years. They have three children and three grandchildren.

Book and Art Order Information

Conversations with Mary

May be ordered through

Your Local Book Store

ISBN # 0-9670406-0-4

or call

1-800-431-1579

————————————————————————

For Pastel Print Orders

Call

1-800-431-1579

Madonna of the	color	22″ x 16″*	**$30.00**
Window (cover)	color	8″ x 5¾″*	**$15.00**
Joy (chapter head)	color	19″ x 13″*	**$25.00**
The Reunion	b&w	8″ x 5¼″*	**$10.00**
The Blessing	b&w	8″ x 5¼″*	**$10.00**
Letting Go	b&w	8″ x 5¼″*	**$10.00**
A Gift of Love	b&w	8″ x 5¼″*	**$10.00**

Set of any three black and white (b&w) prints $25.00

*Note: Dimensions indicate the size of the image.